THE WORLD OF CLOWNS

THE WORLD OF CLOWNS

BY
GEORGE BISHOP

BROOKE HOUSE PUBLISHERS
LOS ANGELES

Library of Congress Cataloging in Publication Data

Bishop, George Victor.
   The world of clowns.

   Bibliography: p.
   1. Clowns—History.   I.   Title.
GV1828.B57   791.3′3′09   76-14989
ISBN 0-912588-29-2

for Patsy

ACKNOWLEDGMENTS

In a book such as this every acknowledgment suggests a score of deserving people and institutions whose names have been omitted. Nevertheless the author would indeed be derelict if he failed to mention the invaluable help and friendship given him by Bobby Kay, a clown. Thanks beyond words are also due Dyer Reynolds for the use of his talent and his vast knowledge of circus lore; to George "Perky" Perkins, a clown; to Shirley Carroll for granting access to the Norman Carroll Circus Collection, now housed in the Los Angeles County Museum of Science and Industry; to Robert L. Parkinson, Librarian and Historian, the Circus World Museum, Baraboo, Wisconsin; to Tom Kelley, whose feeling for clowns is reflected in his photographs; to Gil Porter for his faith in the project; to Jerry Fried for his advice and help; and to Louis Eaton, a publisher who happens to love clowns.

CONTENTS

FOREWORD

Laughter, while it surely will not solve the world's problems, provides us all with a means of relieving tension; and the person best qualified to spread that laughter all over the world is the clown.

As we will see in the following pages, the clown knows no prejudice and has no axe to grind. He is someone that a suspicious and hostile world can turn to for emotional release.

You can trust a clown. He will make you laugh and, in that laughter, give you a chance to pause and see your neighbor, whether he sits across an aisle or an ocean, in a more tolerant light.

Since the middle of the last century, the clown has developed as a peculiarly American institution. He typifies the good things we stand for and his development has, in a curious way, reflected the growth of our own great country.

Now we have a chance to follow him, in words and pictures,

from his very beginnings to the present day and know him more intimately than we have until now.

On a personal level I have never undertaken an assignment that has led me to meet so many generous, warm-hearted people. Clowns have set me at ease and taken me into their homes and dressing-trailers wherever I have traveled to see them. The pleasure of their company is a memory that I shall long cherish.

One final note. A surprising number of individuals—clowns and humans—to whom I have spoken in connection with this volume have suggested that it would be a nice touch to have myself don the motley, be given a face, and so appear in the author's photograph printed on the cover. Although it would be an honor to appear as a clown even in such artificial circumstances, I cannot bring myself to do so; a clown is special and not to be impersonated by a mere mortal. I hope that when the last page of this book is turned, the reader will understand my reticence.

GEORGE BISHOP
Sherman Oaks, California

ENTER
THE
CLOWN

The large two-story room is alive with the colors of toys strewn with planned casualness around its spacious, carpeted floor. The early afternoon California sun streams through the concave glass dome that spans the entire ceiling, bringing a sense of warmth and life to the little groups of children sitting on benches or playing at climbing or crawling games.

Supervising nurses and doctors dressed in sport clothes emphasize the informality that permeates the acute ward of Children's Hospital in Los Angeles. Standing in this bright, inviting room it is difficult to believe that pain and abandoned hope inhabit the small patients' adjoining rooms with a pervasiveness that reasserts itself with stunning finality every time a child dies.

This is a day of great excitement in the acute ward; the circus is in town! Arrangements have been made for all ambulatory cases, including some kids who can manage well in wheelchairs, to be taken in special buses to see the matinee performance. But ambulatory doesn't mean little boys and girls into whose veins constantly drips life-giving intravenous fluid from bottles they tow behind them in little four-wheeled frame carts. (Each cart supports a bottle of clear solution suspended from a single chrome rod and linked to the child's arm by an inserted needle at the end of a plastic tube.) Nor does it mean the bedridden, suffering serious organic or traumatic illnesses. Gradually the floor empties, leaving behind only those unable to go. Somehow the sunshine through the big dome doesn't seem as bright now.

Everyone feels it, the nurses, doctors, and hospital aides left behind even more than the patients; they have seen or will see a circus. The majority of the little ones asking "Why can't I go?" will not, ever.

But something is stirring five floors down in the hospital lobby. The excitement started out in the parking lot where visitors, often guilt-ridden because of their good health and the more somber for it, present a determinedly solemn mien. Much of the sadness is real, reflecting apprehension and loneliness.

Now, impossibly, people are smiling; not only smiling but laughing and nudging one another in appreciation. A crazy, improbable figure wearing a loose-fitting white suit daubed all over with bright colors is making its way along the walkway. A frilly collar around his neck frames a white face featuring a perpetually smiling mouth and topped by a ridiculously tiny conical cap perched saucily between two great tufts of hair; this strange creature, this *clown*, attracts everyone's attention.

After a first startled look at this oddity whose giant webbed feet propel him happily forward, people invariably smile and when the clown smiles back and gives the slightest twitch of a wave with one white-gloved hand he seems magically to flick away the care and worry in the face of each passerby.

And what does he see, this clown, as he makes his way toward the acute ward five stories up?

Our clown sees no strangers, only friends anxious to share his infectious joy. It is as though he moves surrounded by an unseen aura the invisible touch of which converts cynic into believer and vindictiveness into compassion, if only for the moment. The eyes of a clown are like magic prisms absorbing the realities and separating them so that menace and ill-will are filtered out to leave only goodness, kindness, and tolerance in view.

A clown sees a world devoid of suspicion or mistrust; he views the world as guilelessly as a young child, a world of outgoing friendliness that seeks only friendliness in return. And instinctively we know it, and gladly offer that friendliness.

The funny makeup and costume are a big part of it, of course, because they remove a clown from reality. He's not going to steal your wife, take your job, rob you, menace your children, or cause you discomfort by being of another race or espousing a different creed. A clown is a political, social, and economic neuter. He contradicts everything we have come to expect in these "cynical seventies." He doesn't return good for evil; he knows no evil. He represents a trustworthy escape from a burdensome pattern of personal and national crisis. We can abandon our insecurities, doubts, and suspicions in his presence; he will not take advantage of our temporary emotional vulnerability; he will never let us down.

A clown sees life simply, without complications. Something hurts—he cries. Something pleases him—he laughs. Something puzzles him—he frowns. Something frightens him—he runs. His exaggerated reactions are basic and straightforward. Why, we ask ourselves, can't *life* be that simple? Well, at least for a few minutes, it can, and we are grateful.

I do not know what makes a clown, how he or she arrives at that particular stage of development where, suddenly, *voilà*, there is a clown. I certainly don't believe that eight weeks of training in a clown school makes a clown. The best I can do in these pages is to try to explain how the American clown, so different from painted and costumed performers elsewhere in the world, came into being, and hopefully to have you experience the uplifting, overwhelming sense of elation that comes from knowing him even a little bit.

Come see yourself through the eyes of a clown. No anger, resentment, or frustration shows on your face. That dubious frown doesn't quite make it to your forehead. Despite yourself, despite all your painfully acquired emotional shields, you fight back a smile. The battle is soon decided. You smile reluctantly, then less grudgingly, then, finally, because you *want* to. Your smile feels good and so obviously pleases the clown that you smile again until your laughter sends him into a paroxysm of pantomime rapture. You are playing his game, now. He knows that you're looking for a good excuse to let yourself go and he gladly, flamboyantly supplies it.

That's what our clown is doing now! Look at him performing for the nurses and parents in the elevator. The tiny room is a cage of laughter. The visitors, despite their private sadness, are convulsed by his antics. That nurse was intending to get off at the third floor, but somehow she missed it. Whatever the reason she's along for the ride now, all the way to the fifth.

As the elevator with its happy passengers ascends, let us take a closer look at our clown and clowns everywhere. Let's try to find out what sparks this character, this *clown,* why we like him, instinctively, as much as we do, and why he makes us like ourselves.

THE
WAY IT
WAS

When William Shakespeare had Hamlet advise the players who came to Elsinore not to let their "clowns speak more than is set down for them," he was really chastising his good friend William Kempe, who happened to be a clown. Shakespeare had appeared with Kempe when both were actors in the Lord Chamberlain's Company; the two are on record as being paid for performances at Court on December 26 and 27, 1594.

The time-honored author's lament to the actor, "Just read the lines, don't ad-lib," was given Hamlet to say because Shakespeare, when he began writing plays, often included a clownish part for Kempe. The two Dromios, the two Gobbos, Launce and Speed, Costard and Dull, were probably written as comic parts for his actor friend and a new partner. Unfortunately Kempe was something of an extrovert and took to embellishing the Bard's lines with little bits of business and stories of his own. Hence Shakespeare's indirect admonition to stick to the script.

The tradition of the clown comedy team as envisioned by Shakespeare has continued through the intervening centuries, going from Costard and Dull, to Tabarin and Mondor in France, Punch and Judy in England, George L. Fox and Tony Denier in nineteenth-century America, and, more recently, to Abbott and Costello and Rowan and Martin. Through three centuries the functions of clown and comic have separated as the clown lost his voice and the comic his bizarre makeup and costume.

Looking back through history the clown may be seen as one of the first true citizens of the world. Perhaps some new scroll will be uncovered that will identify the clown's place in the Assyrian or Egyptian life-style, but for now the joking acrobatic bands traveling through the Greek countryside in the era of the city-states will do as our clown starting point. The revelers celebrated the grape harvest by performing impromptu skits with improvised dialogue and relied heavily on what we would now call slapstick routines. Aristophanes in his light parody *Frogs* wrote what may be the first true clown part in literature. Bacchus, his clown character, takes his servant down with him to a place of departed spirits, and the ser-

vant's terrified reaction provides the elemental humor of the piece.

But we really have to span the dark ages and look to the Renaissance to establish the internationalism of the performer as he has evolved into our present-day American clown. In the sixteenth and seventeenth centuries strolling minstrel companies, at times numbering forty or more, each having twelve or thirteen actors and actresses, played the length and breadth of the dozens of independent principalities and fiefdoms we now call Italy. Born, as were their much earlier Greek counterparts, from improvised sketches and dialogues of peasants celebrating the grape harvest, the routines of these players soon established certain type-cast parts that included at least two clowns.

From these companies we first hear of clown types such as Arlecchino, a stupid, dull country lout who evolved into the brisk and lively Harlequin of the English pantomime. And Pulcinella, a Neapolitan clod, became the light comedy Polichinelle of France and then, finally, the irresistible English puppet-show renegade, Punch. Pedrolino, originally a country bumpkin, gradually became the poetic, pathetic Pierrot, one of the most celebrated clowns to shift the emphasis of his performance, playing for sympathetic tears rather than the unrestrained laughter of his Latin antecedents.

Tabarin, a seventeenth-century French clown, probably epitomizes the transition from the talking, acrobatic clown to the wisecracking modern team comics. He was the most famous jack-pudding of France. Today Dick Martin of Rowan and Martin would be called a jack-pudding, the fellow who though seemingly not too bright always tops his partner or "feeder" and gets most of the laughs. Tabarin's feeder was a French patent-medicine salesman named Mondor, and the two set up shop at one end of the Pont-Neuf in Paris. Their act consisted of Mondor pitching all manner of esoteric remedies for every imaginable ill and Tabarin getting his laughs by deliberately misunderstanding his "master" and turning the quack doctor's words against him. Tabarin and Mondor would have felt very at home on a television variety show that features the quick-cuts and fast one-liners used by many contemporary comedy teams.

Pulcinella, a Neapolitan clown, who surfaced in the sixteenth century, is a vital link between Greek and Roman players and the modern-day descendants of the English Punch. As developed by wandering performers, his costume and face gradually evolved through hunchback and pot belly into the loose-fitting garment we identify with the whiteface clown.

Gradually the clown concept has come full circle, beginning with the rough-and-tumble, agile buffoon whose locally tailored jests enlivened the wine festivals, through the more sophisticated pantomime of England's Joseph Grimaldi (from whom the clown nickname "Joey" stems) to the present-day circus clown working, as did his Greek predecessor more than two thousand years ago, as a "single" relying on his own ability to provoke laughter.

No book devoted to the American clown would be complete without a few words about Joseph Grimaldi. His father, Giuseppe Grimaldi, was one of a group of itinerant Italian players who tried their luck in France and Britain. The pantomime—the word, of Greek origin, means "the imitator of all things"—was in vogue in England, with the thrust of the word changed from a reference to a specific individual (The Pantomime) to the play in which he performed.

Grimaldi senior was hired by English stage actor and manager David Garrick to perform in his Drury Lane theatre as a mime. He was an immediate success, with the *London Chronicle* critic writing: "Grimaldi is a man of great strength and agility; he indeed treads the air . . . If he has any fault he is rather too comical." Grimaldi gradually changed the interpretation of his role in the pantomime away from the more stylish and graceful English Harlequin to the earlier Italian Punchinello concept which, ironically, is the modern forerunner of what we think of as the American circus clown.

The English writer Joseph Addison describes Grimaldi's Harlequin: "Harlequin's part is made up of blunders and absurdities. He is to mistake one name for another; forget his errands, to stumble over queans (girls) and to run against every post that comes his way." Surely Lou Jacobs or Emmett Kelly would recognize that description.

Joseph Grimaldi, born on December 18, 1779, appeared at age two on the stage of England's Sadler's Wells dressed as a clown, an exact miniature reproduction of his father's costume. As he grew older he appeared as a midget clown and as a monkey with his father. A story has it that clowning nearly led to his early death when, appearing as a monkey and being whirled around violently

by his father on the end of a chain, a link parted sending him crashing into the first row of stall seats below.

It was Joseph Grimaldi who first began looking like the clown as we know him today. Although he did not in the beginning use whiteface, he did daub patches of red on his face to achieve a mischievous look and his white costume was covered in spangles and sewn-on colored silk patches. He also hopped around a lot and, as a talking clown, had a rich, clear, singing voice that appealed hugely to the theatergoers. Called "The Michelangelo of buffoonery" by a contemporary, the original Joey had an impact best described by Andrew Halliday, a nineteenth-century writer: "He trusted to all the force of his natural humor; and such was his power that he made a success of pieces which were utterly wanting even in the commonest accessories of spectacle." What clown would not want those words for his epitaph?

Makeup in one form or another has been a part of clowning since the very beginning. Understanding the need physically to separate their characters from reality, the earliest Greek and Latin "vintage" comics daubed their faces with the juice of the grape to fix a mask between themselves and ordinary mortals. The very word *mask* stems from the Arabic *masharage,* meaning "clown." The sooted cheeks of the English sidewalk entertainer, the red nose of the unsteady imbiber, the bismuth forerunner of clown white used by Grimaldi, the current elaborate faces seen elsewhere in these pages, all point up the necessity of neutralizing a clown.

To be successful a clown must be essentially sexless. The "clownperson" of the newly sanitized language form will not do. A clown is not a "he" or "she" or even a "person." That's why the readily identifiable female clown being turned out by clown schools is disturbing to many enthusiasts. As soon as one looks at a clown and says, "That's a girl," all is lost. She may as well strip off her clothes, remove her greasepaint, and cavort in the altogether.

True, we refer to a clown as "he" in this book, but only as a common term of reference that will not distract the reader. "She" would certainly bring us up sharp at every use and "it," though

The 1943 Clyde Beatty show featured (from left) Hughie Kyle, Mark Anthony, Kenneth Waite, Perky, a sailor whiteface, Billy Burke, Art Larue, and Del LeClair.

The entire clown contingent of the 1940 Cole Brothers Circus includes a rare picture of tramp Otto Griebling (third from right, bottom row) in whiteface. (Left to right, top row seated): Karl De Motte, Albert White, Harold Hall, Jack Klippel.
(Middle row): Lawrence Cross, Rube Simmons, Leonard Pearson, Bobby Kay.
(Bottom row): Arthur Borella, Danny McBride, Lee Smith, Bill Bailey, Happy Holmes, Otto Griebling, Horace Laird, Dennis Stevens.

perhaps ideal in a striving toward objectivity, hardly projects the humanness and warmth that is the very heart of our subject.

How does the clown vary so widely yet stay the same through so many centuries and in such different situations? Fifty-one years ago Brander Mathews, writing in *The Mentor,* put it this way:

"Whatever its variations the type abides. The clown, now, as in the remotest past of which we have any record, is sometimes brilliant and sometimes blundering. Sometimes with characteristic inconsistency he is both brilliant and blundering, each in its turn; and while he makes us laugh he may be ready to weep as soon as we leave him alone with his real self.

"It will not do to dwell too much, however, on the infrequent case of the clown being other than he seems. He is not generally a melancholy creature . . . Laughter is what we need, and it matters little to most of us whether he who supplies it be as light-hearted as he appears or as heavy-hearted as we may suspect. That is the function of the clown, whatever part he may play, whatever name he may be called by, whatever absurd attire he may deck himself in—to supply laughter, the laughter which is as necessary to man as digestion and sleep. The part of the clown in the economy of life is a more important one than some of us realize."

A point well taken and nowhere better illustrated than in our present troubled times. It is possible that the American clown, once thought doomed when the big shows struck their canvas and clown living-trailers sprouted television antennas, is emerging as he has done in other forms centuries past as a welcome refuge from reality, an emotional catharsis to restore our sense of personal priorities.

"Laughter is the surest touch of genius in creation," writes Christopher Fry in *The Lady's Not For Burning.* How did this touch of clown genius take form in this country to implant itself indelibly in the American ethos? As much as anywhere it began with a man named George L. Fox.

GEORGE L. FOX

George L. Fox, the first great American whiteface. A study by Dyer Reynolds.

The often-held concept that beneath a clown's façade of gaiety and humor lies a deep personal melancholy, although in the main ill-founded, appears to have applied in the case of the first widely acclaimed classical white-face American clown, George L. Fox. Born in 1825, he achieved nationwide popularity before he died under tragic circumstances.

It might be well now to consider the early relationship between clown, circus, and theater to explain why the first great American clown was essentially a theatrical performer. In a sense, with the big shows now no longer under canvas and appearing in large arenas around the country, the circus—like the clown—has come full circle. The early nineteenth-century American circus often consisted of nothing more than one elephant traveling from town to town being exhibited in the largest available local barn. Such was the starvation of rural, frontier America for diversion of any kind that the arrival of the "advance man," hired by the elephant's owner to keep one or two days ahead of the "show" posting billboards, would signal a general migration from farms for miles around.

By the middle eighteen-hundreds it was plain that where an elephant, tiger, or camel could attract good business, a real show featuring both animal and human performers would do much better. Soon the country was being crisscrossed by scores of mud shows, small one-ring affairs so called because their two or three wagons often needed local help to free themselves from muddy roads and fields. The competition was fierce, with one show frequently tearing down the opposition's "paper"—colored posters announcing its arrival—and not above burning a bridge behind it so that the following show had to detour many miles to cross a river or stream.

The smaller shows featured a single ring, some trained horses and riders, and not much else; sometimes they carried a "strong man" to challenge local talent, and perhaps a belly dancer who, for a small extra fee, performed her tortile gyrations in an enclosure between two wagons. Even the five Ringling Brothers began very modestly in 1882. According to an unknown observer, "They started with a handful of actors, three horses, a tent that would not seat

Otto Griebling, considered by many to be the finest carpet-tramp ever to work under canvas.

more than six-hundred people and a half-score of farm wagons, to which hired teams were hitched."

The clown act was one feature that separated the larger circuses from the early mud shows. The circus clown as we know him in this country today first made his appearance as a journeyman time killer, more of a necessity than an added luxury to attract more customers. The first clown was called the carpet clown, as he still is today, and is perhaps the one true indigenous American clown. His name and function came to him this way:

Almost from the very beginning the bareback riders were the royalty of the circus. Horses were readily available, hardy on the road, and relatively easy to train. The spectacle of a man or woman in skin-tight costume performing all manner of gymnastics on the back of a prancing, saddleless horse thrilled yokel and city-dweller alike, and what began as the only act of a one-ring show quickly evolved into the star attraction of the three-ring circus.

From 1890 through 1945—the golden age of the circus—the often mile-long parade of animals, cages, and performers from a railroad siding to the newly erected big top was an essential feature of the big, sometimes hundred-railroad-car shows. The circus had come a long way, literally and figuratively, since 1856 when Spalding and Rogers first put their wagons on flat cars and moved their show by rail. The parade advertised the product, whetting appetites for the wonders that would soon be on display in the sideshow and animal tents, to say nothing of the show itself under the big top. The bareback riders were the only performers aside from the male aerialists to be excused from the parade. The long bareback ride proved too demanding on their thigh muscles and knees, making them unable to perform properly in the center ring.

The male aerialists or "flyers" were excused only because they were needed to supervise the vital placing of the high-wire and trapeze rigging. Unlike the equestrians' theirs was not an absence permitted because of the nature of their performance; *female* flyers had to attend the parade. Interestingly enough, when the big shows toured Europe the traditional parade had to be abandoned. Europeans, bred on much smaller, less colorful circuses, flocked to see

the unloading and parade, then went home certain that nothing more spectacular could possibly be presented under canvas!

The early circus that featured trick riders and several other performing animal acts did not function with the split-second precision of present-day shows. When there were only two rings, equipment from a previous act had to be cleared before a new performance could begin. Since the music was at most rudimentary, consisting of a drum and one or two brass instruments, entertainment had to be provided during the action lapses.

Enter the carpet clown. He had certain definite needs as far as dress and makeup were concerned. He couldn't follow the traditional whiteface because he performed in all kinds of weather, took pratfalls, hung on the horses' tails, and generally got dirty all over, which excluded the frilly, white, sequined conventional clown costume as well.

So the carpet clown kept his own face but used reds and blacks and pinks to mark him as a clown and to give him something other than a human character; his costume usually consisted of dark, tattered trousers and jacket with scruffy shoes and some kind of misshapen hat. The outfit was loose-fitting and practical; the more it got banged up during the act the more authentically "trampish" he looked, badgering the other performers or threatening the ringmaster with mayhem, using an exaggerated imitation of the master's whip.

Why "carpet"? The all-important bareback riders often had to work in wet weather, either without any cover at all or sheltered by a leaky, torn piece of canvas. Since their footing was vital to their safety, they always laid a carpet down in the ring where they worked so that when they jumped on and off the horses their resined feet were sure to grip the woven surface rather than skid treacherously on mud or wet grass. Hence the lowly carpet clown began as a workhorse time-filler until he finally emerged as a star in the persons of such great circus tramps as Otto Griebling and Emmett Kelly or Red Skelton in his television portrayals.

The carpet clown had one privilege that set him apart from his fellows. Normally, the ringmaster was the absolute monarch of all he surveyed; even the bareback riders deferred to his shrill whistle that terminated one act and called on its successor. The clowns, low in the circus pecking order to begin with, were especially at his mercy because their routines could quickly be terminated with some bit of foolishness that brought a laugh and left the audience none the wiser. If the performance was running long, the splendidly attired gentleman with the imperious manner would yank off the clowns, and they would docilely grab their props and run for the exit as though their lives, or at least their jobs, depended on it.

But not the carpet clown. Because if the show ran *short*, if one act was late in setting up or some accident halted the show, the ringmaster had to call on him. There he sat through each performance, usually perched disconsolately on the edge of one of the rings, morosely watching the action. He needed no signal from the ringmaster but sprang into action when he saw something go wrong. Often his distractions, such as getting involved with a balancing act and falling a lot or elaborately pantomiming a juggler and dropping everything, left the circus fan unaware that there was any lag in the action. And the crowd loved it most when the clown approached the ringmaster, aping his movements, issuing orders in pantomime and generally assaulting his dignity. But they couldn't share the carpet clown's private glee or know that his target's rage was more real than feigned.

At the time of George L. Fox, however, in the middle 1800s, the still-small circus was no place for a clown seeking star stature. He turned naturally, as did his European counterpart, to the stage. Fox came from a theatrical family. Like England's Joseph Grimaldi, to whom he was often compared, he started young, making his first public appearance on a Boston stage when he was only five. He appeared in legitimate roles, playing Phineas Fletcher in *Uncle Tom's Cabin* in New York in 1853. He became closely associated with the role of Humpty Dumpty in a ten-week run at the Olympic Theatre and eventually played the role 1,268 times in New York alone.

But Tony Pastor's famous Bowery Theatre gave the comic clown some of his greatest challenges. He teamed up with Tony Denier for a time but soon went back on his own as a headliner at

Red Skelton. A motion picture or television clown must never hide his identity behind his face.

Dan Rice—more comedian than clown.

Pastor's. Today's clown has it easy compared with the audiences Fox faced. Bowery Theatre-goers took their clowns seriously and the relationship between performer and customer was very personal. One episode illustrates what being a clown meant in 1870 in New York.

Fox was the headliner on a bill that also included a female clown named Fanny Herring. Fanny had her following, but there was no doubt that it was Fox's presence that packed the theater night after night. The first signs of what would become a fatal illness had begun to manifest themselves and the great clown often worked in some pain as the headaches that later led to apparent brain damage plagued him.

Backstage, Fanny, who admired Fox, would imitate him for the rest of the cast, copying his movements with amazing accuracy. One night Fox's pain got the best of him, making it impossible for him to go on. The manager was faced with a sold-out house; Fanny Herring persuaded him to let her do Fox's act without informing the patrons. Fox used a very severe, "neat" whiteface makeup adapted from the classical European style, and Fanny, a natural mimic, got through part of the first act without any problems.

Unhappily Fanny was blessed with only one good eye, a fact known and accepted by her fans when she was doing her own act. However, impersonating someone else, especially a big name, was another matter. Word soon spread among the gallery regulars that it was "The Herring" and not "The Fox" on stage. During intermission several stout lads legged it over to a nearby fish market, purchased several dozen smoked herrings, and promptly gouged one eye out of each fish.

When Fanny, flushed with her first-act triumph, reappeared, she was met by a barrage of one-eyed namesakes and retreated in disorder, never again, it is said, to imitate the great clown even backstage.

Fox's last known performance was as his beloved Humpty Dumpty on the stage at New York's Booth Theatre on November 25, 1875. According to a contemporary his mental problems were showing in his performance and he looked "the saddest, saddest clown that ever chalked his face." He never again appeared in public and died in an asylum two years later at the age of fifty-two.

A story, possibly apocryphal, sums up the tortured life of George L. Fox. At the height of his fame a patient supposedly went to a physician and complained of persistent depression. The medical doctor examined him and could find nothing organically wrong. Finally, after several visits during which the patient's melancholy grew progressively worse, the doctor decided to try what we would now call psychological therapy. "Why don't you take an evening off and go see George L. Fox?" the physician suggested. The patient looked at him for a moment, then replied, "I am Fox." True or not the story seems to be in keeping with the clown's tragic ending.

Dan Rice, another performer of that era, is often thought of as being Fox's equal if not his superior in his ability to entertain. While it is true that Rice gained enormous popularity, it is also true that he was more vaudeville performer than clown. He did not "chalk his face" in the classic tradition. Indeed his lanky frame and long beard are said to have inspired the universal likeness of "Uncle Sam" as we know him today, a far cry from a clown concept. Rice was a prolific performer. He is credited with the introduction to the United States of the Pete Jenkins act, an adaptation of the English Tailor's Ride to Brentford.

In the Jenkins act, later made famous by the trick-riding clown Poodles Hanneford, an apparently drunken rube would emerge from the circus audience, challenging the ringmaster to let him ride a seemingly balky horse in place of the previously announced "ill" star performer. The ringmaster would reluctantly agree and, after doing everything wrong and sending the crowd into hysterics with his clumsy tactics, the rube would suddenly master the art and give a breathless display of trick riding that was greeted by stunned applause.

Rice also used trained animals, notably a hog named Lord Byron who could spell out words by nudging letter-cards with his snout. George "Perky" Perkins was later to have a similar success with a fox named Mickey, said to be the only one of its species to perform in a clown act. Perky used Mickey during the walk-around, that part of the show where all the clowns move around the track, pausing from time to time to do their specialties. Perky would come out carrying a rifle, obviously hunting. The object of his search lay curled up in his hat, staring unconcernedly out at a laughing audience. The producing clown, who made many of the gag props used by himself and others during his more than forty-year career, recalls that Mickey was such a smash hit that the other clowns on the Cole Brothers show begged him to leave the fox out of his act; they were getting too little reaction to their own routines!

Rice, whose real name was Daniel McLaren, took his stage name from the famous Irish clown, Dan Rice. The Uncle Sam image attracted the attention of Abraham Lincoln, who invited the performer to the White House and encouraged him in the characterization. Rice entertained Union troops during the Civil War, using Lord Byron as a morale builder in an act where, as Rice sang a popular song, "Root, Hog, or Die!" his porcine lordship would daintily select an American flag from a varied assortment, then parade around with it in his mouth.

A former jockey, the nimble, imaginative Rice did a vaudeville act as Uncle Sam in the Lecture Room—really a theater disguised to remove the stigma then attached to the stage—in P. T. Barnum's famous New York Museum.

Facts about Rice's life are hard to come by. He earned either "the then fabulous salary of $35,000 a year," according to Hal Oliver in a 1944 magazine article, or the astronomical "$100,000 a year" reported by Irving Wallace in his book *The Fabulous Showman,* published in 1959; he counted "Robert E. Lee among his best friends" (Wallace), or "was Abraham Lincoln's favorite" (as reported by John Culhane in *The New York Times*); he died "broke and embittered, a ward of New Jersey relatives, in his seventy-seventh year"

Reading from top to bottom: Mickey and Perky on the Cole Brothers Circus, 1944.

(Wallace), or he "died in 1892, at the age of eighty-four (and) preserved his mentality and cheerfulness to the end" (according to the more contemporaneous Robert Edmund Sherwood in his book *Here We Go Again,* published in 1926).

Perhaps it is fitting that this clown who was not quite a clown should retain a certain mythical quality; after all, clowns are not real people and should not be expected to sully their essential innocence by conforming to human standards.

THE
LEARNING
YEARS

lowning is an evolutionary art. No one really knows where different types of clown faces came from; they simply evolved as the result of a kind of greasepaint Darwinism. If you didn't adapt, change your face, alter your style, learn to "go big" and "play high," and to use your face and costume to maximum advantage, you simply didn't survive. Practically the only thing that the modern American clown has in common with his seventeenth- and eighteenth-century European counterpart is the fact that they both use some foreign matter on their faces to alter their appearance.

Even trying to establish a reasoning process in the evolution of a single clown's face over a thirty-year period is doomed to failure. What great clowns like Lou Jacobs and Bobby Kay looked like twenty-five years ago bears little similarity to their established present-day faces. They experimented, often drastically, until *they got the proper reaction.* That is what clowning is all about; perhaps more than any other form of entertainment, clown humor has a gut-to-gut relationship between performer and audience; there are few subtleties of staging or lighting to interfere with the raw communion of cause and effect.

In the old days of vaudeville when the six-month May-October circus season was over, clowns who wanted to work during the winter could find bookings on the stage that would keep them busy until spring. As vaudeville died out, that source of revenue dried up and most clowns who earned an average of twenty-five to thirty dollars a week plus their keep in the circus during the thirties and forties could not make it through the winter on their savings. Star clowns such as Bobby Kay, Mark Anthony, Otto Griebling, and Lou Jacobs might make anywhere from three to five hundred a week by the fifties and sixties, but the big salaries were the exception and did not reflect the average clown's earnings.

As television became a major source of entertainment in the fifties and sixties, the mud shows found the going rough, the medium-sized circuses either merged or sold out to the one or two remaining big shows, and the long apprenticeship at very nominal wages that produced succeeding generations of clowns ceased to

Lou Jacobs on the left with Paul Jerome, both internationally known clowns photographed in the late 1930s. Compare Jacobs's face with the contemporary study by Dyer Reynolds in color.

Paul Jung, legendary whiteface who initiated many of the popular clown rou-tines, stands atop his wagon living-quarters with the Clyde Beatty Circus in 1941.

interest young people accustomed to higher earnings in other branches of show business. To the exhortation "Bring on the clowns!" circus management increasingly cried out in despair, "From where?" True, with the reduction of traveling shows the need for clowns decreased, but the one remaining big circus not only stretched the season from six to nine months but operated two shows—a "red" and a "blue" unit—simultaneously, requiring the services of fifty or sixty clowns.

One answer to the scarcity was the creation of a clown school eight years ago. In theory the school was the obvious remedy for both the lack of a natural training ground and the need to pay beginning clowns a wage that at least approached what they could make as performers in other media.

First begun as a publicity stunt, the school has snowballed into an annual $200,000 investment. The circus, committed to the precipitate incubation of young clowns, is forced to keep feeding untried graduates into the arena. "A better idea," suggests Shirley Carroll who, with her late husband Norman, for many years publicized the circus, "would have been to apprentice the youngsters to the older clowns. Instead of downgrading the veterans and ending up with nothing, the circus would have had at least as much publicity and the public interest would have been piqued to watch the learning teams at work."

The American Guild of Variety Artists organized the clowns and negotiated a base pay of $185.00 per week. Old-timers still working viewed the unionization with mixed feelings. Many now in their middle sixties or early seventies (clowns have an amazing longevity) had toiled forty years without getting that much money and, while grateful for their salary raise, resented the fact that people who had never before worked an audience received the same pay. In addition, circus publicity tried to cash in on its own brainchild by touting the youngsters' supposed superiority.

Each year the clown school conducts a series of regional auditions and selects fifty applicants for an intensive eight-week course in Venice, Florida. The would-be clowns are exposed to everything from basic ballet to makeup to pratfall techniques, with the twenty

Three famous clowns ham it up backstage on the Ringling show in the late 1930s. From the left, Joe Lewis, Paul Jung, and Paul Jerome.

A close-up study of Joe Lewis, one of the first prominent cop clowns. The straight lines above and below his eyes and the three short dashes at the corners show the still prevalent '30s influence of the European whiteface.

or so annual graduates offered contracts with the circus. Although this would seem a natural way to replenish the dwindling supply of clowns, circus insiders privately admit that the costly experiment has been something less than a success.

"They think the world owes them a living," one veteran clown told me. "They put on a face and costume, go through the motions, and think they're clowns. They spend more time arguing for their supposed employment rights than doing their job." While admittedly somewhat prejudiced, the old-school clown pointed up the reason for the clown school's failure without perhaps fully realizing its implications. That the clown school was not turning out an acceptable product was dramatically brought home in 1974 when, in mid-season, the circus summarily fired fifteen clowns. This serious denuding of an important part of the show would not have occurred without extreme provocation, ranging from lack of discipline on the circus train to slipshod performance. The sleeping cars (each clown now has his own compartment) were, according to one observer, "turning into whorehouses," a reference to some clowns' penchant for entertaining female performers during overnight jumps. Although, in today's permissive society, not at first blush a serious condition, the offending clowns easygoing life style carried over into their work. They would walk through their acts, conveying none of the warmth and desire to amuse that are the essential attributes of a successful circus clown.

To understand why today's production-line clowns, with relatively few exceptions—perhaps ten percent of clown-school graduates over the past eight years have really made good in the circus— have failed in their craft, we must take a look at how things were in the 1930s when the big top, the side show, and the animal tent were at the height of their flag-bedecked, boisterous glory.

Back in those days the circus carried an incredible eight hundred workingmen—*roustabouts* to the outsider—just to handle the canvas and equipment and to care for the animals. Average pay was $3.50 per week with room and board supplied as well as, in some cases, working clothes by the wardrobe department. But the food was good and plentiful and for a man of little education in those

Uncle Heavy and his trained pigs are natural clowns on the Ken Jensen show in 1951.

depression-ridden times the circus provided travel and security in exchange for manual labor, a not uneven compact.

In the circus's rigid social structure the clowns, while a cut above the workingmen, shared with the cowboys and Indians the lowest perch in the performers' pecking order. Sleeping accommodations tell the story. A starting clown—that is, someone willing to learn the craft for all the workingman's perquisites minus the $3.50 per week—was assigned to a three-high double at the beginning of his nearly six-month train journey. Consisting of three berths stacked one over the other and each containing two people, the three-high soon tested the embryonic clown's dedication. It was impossible to sit up in the berths, one simply rolled in, often alongside a complete stranger given the nomadic ways of performers during those days, slept the night with no light and little air, then rolled out again in the morning.

The crowded conditions provided great incentive for the aspiring performer. A regular spot in the show, even if it involved only a walk-around during the opening spectacular or anchoring the bottom of a rope for a climbing flyer, earned him assignment to a two-high double and the professional status that accompanied such spacious accommodations. After a year or two the successful clown was given a single upper, usually in lieu of a salary increase, and stardom was marked by a single lower with access to the window, where even the soot that entered through a screened air vent was infinitely more desirable than the upper where, as one old-timer remarked, "You got nothin' but feet."

In going through these larval stages the immature, frightened, uncertain young man who rolled into the top tier of his first three-high double evolved into the full beauty and perfection of a circus clown radiating from within the joy of his calling. His evolution was a slow, sometimes painful process with older, established clowns more often than not jealously guarding their secrets, hindering rather than aiding upstarts who seemed a threat to their primacy.

"In those days," Otto Griebling observed, "you not only had to learn, you had to learn *hard.*" Griebling, a carpet-tramp clown, was considered by his peers to be an outstanding performer. Often confused in the public mind with Emmett Kelly, Griebling lacked Kelly's business acumen and flair for publicity. A story is told that when Kelly was just starting out he would take half his meager salary every payday and give it to a publicist, an unheard-of ploy for a circus clown in the 1930s. The circus wanted no star clown because that meant a higher salary, but such was Kelly's sense of theater that people began coming to see him do things that they had been conditioned to look for by judiciously planted press releases.

Soon, like a baseball player upon whom the press has bestowed a charismatic mantle, Kelly's presence in the hippodrome guaranteed more tickets sold, and his salary soared past that of any other clown before or since. At his peak Griebling earned five hundred dollars per week, a goodly sum but according to his contemporaries far below fair compensation for his talents; while Kelly, semi-retired as of this writing (clowns retire only when they die) commanded fifteen hundred per week during his last circus years.

Both Griebling and Kelly learned their craft the hard way, and the question of who was the more talented, guaranteed to provoke a lively argument in any clown gathering, is beside the point. What present-day circus owners must ask themselves is "Where are the clowns of the future?" It is a question that cannot be answered here; rather we can take delight in delving into circus lore and reliving the great traditions that created that unique entertainment phenomenon, the American clown.

Between shows. Three weary famous tramps caught off guard. (Left to right): Otto Griebling, Emmett Kelly, Gene Randow.

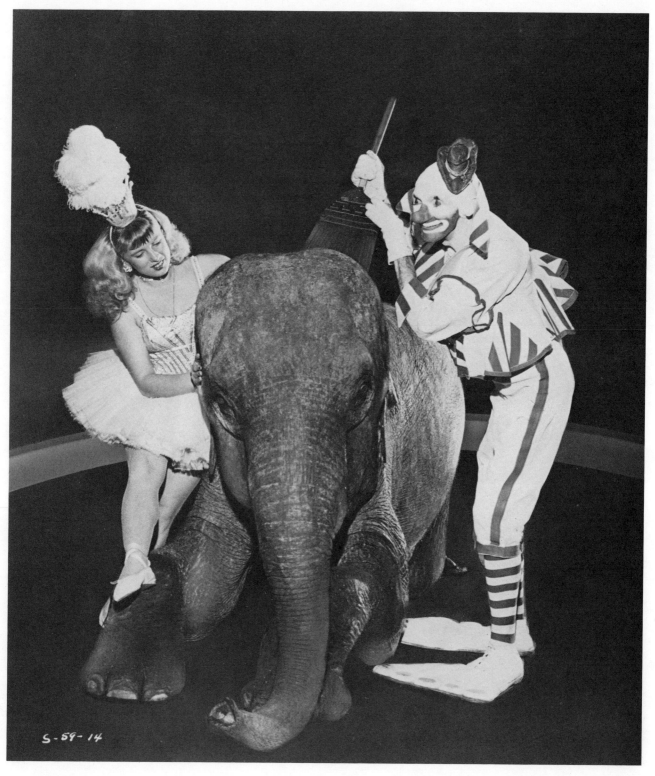

S-59-14

There is more than one way to skin—or pretty up—an elephant. Gene Lewis and equestrienne Evy Karoly show how it's done in the center ring.

Backstage, trainer Walter McClain uses a blowtorch to get rid of that five-o'clock shadow before showtime.

5
CLOWN ALLEY

espite the fact that P.T. Barnum once said that "Clowns and elephants are the two pegs that you hang the circus on," the importance of the human half of that formula was not always readily apparent behind the scenes. It took stamina and dedication to become a clown; perhaps that's why the men and women who made it were so good at their calling: anything won that dearly must surely have at least a touch of excellence.

When a big circus put up its canvas, one large tent was set back from public view and given over to feeding the twelve hundred or more performers and workingmen traveling with the show; a second was reserved as a dressing area. The division of this second tent never varied through six months of moving from place to place; it tells us a great deal about the status of the circus clowns.

Pull back the entrance flap and look in first on the paddock room. The *pad* consisted of a center space containing the riding-acts' horses' equipment at one end and the wardrobe room at the other. This practical arrangement allowed riders in elaborate, often cumbersome costumes to don them and mount their horses in one place, ready for one of the *specs*—the spectaculars that opened and closed every show. All female performers dressed behind canvas on the left side of the pad while male performers used the right side.

In the men's dressing area one entered from the pad onto "Broadway," an open corridor running the full length of the tent that permitted some "walking-around room" for performers from the cramped makeup areas. The next row to Broadway, a choice location because there was no one down one side of you, was occupied by the flyers and bareback riders. The second row of folding canvas chairs, makeup tables, and mirrors was allotted to the aerial stationary-bar performers and the solo trapeze artists. The third row (the air began to get a little heavy as one moved farther in) was inhabited by wire-walkers, jugglers, liberty horse workers—who walked around the ring directing riderless horses with whip flicks and voice commands—and manage or house riders. These latter, supposedly skilled equestrians, were quite often pressed into service from other departments to provide warm bodies in the saddles of trained horses. "Just clamp your knees tight and hold on," a worried chimp handler would be advised. "The horse knows the act better than you do." And off he would go, elegantly costumed and hanging on for dear life, while his mount did the complicated circles and crossovers with twenty or more of his stallmates and no one in the audience the wiser. Other circus folk took to referring to these unhappy surrogates as "manage riders, because they just manage to stay on."

The mess tent under canvas. Clowns were always given first seating because their elaborate makeup takes so much time.

Then, in the fourth but not the last row, came the clowns. This row has often mistakenly been referred to as "Clown Alley," though the phrase has quite a different origin. The clown, more than any other performer, depends on elaborate facial makeup. His face is, quite literally, his fortune. Although veteran clowns putting on their faces in fifteen or twenty minutes make the whole exercise appear effortless, years of practice and fine adjustment of markings and color lie behind every successful clown face.

The basic ingredients are simple. First a layer of "clown white"—a paste the consistency of putty each clown once mixed himself using rectified zinc oxide and any Crisco-like substance, that now comes ready-made in jars—is applied, covering all skin on the face and neck that will show. If it is applied too thinly, the pinkish skin color will leak through; if too thickly, it will come up white-white and form more of a mask than a face. The base is gently powdered before the colors are put on. Then, after the colors are applied, the major powdering, using a sock crammed with white talc, occurs. This involves "beating yourself to death" with the sock on the grease base that comes up in tiny tacky points to hold the powder; this operation cleats on the color and white very firmly so that the face will hold for as long as twelve hours.

This self-beating process sends up a thin white cloud to hover in the air and settle on the clothes of adjoining artistes. When a clown forgetfully performs this ritual at his trunk, cries of "Get out into the alley" arise from all sides and the contrite clown skips down to a small open space at the end of the makeup row set aside for just that purpose. That open space, not the actual makeup row, became known as "Clown Alley." A clown's hearing deteriorates as the season progresses because the powder keeps building up in the natural earwax until it finally forms a hard ball that must be removed by a medical doctor.

The clown's trunk is both the badge and tool of his profession. No other trunk is quite like it. Zinc-lined across the bottom and a foot or so up the sides to sit dry on the most waterlogged ground, it is his wardrobe, makeup case, and vanity all compressed by necessity and experience into the area of a regular steamer trunk. Open

Frankie Saluto lends an ear to Prince Paul. Midget clowns have become as indispensable a part of many classic routines as a clown and his trunk.

Midget clown Mike Padillo plays it "straight" as he tows water-skiing Lou Jacobs through the walk- or roll-around. Keeping the "skis" pointed straight and staying upright with seeming effortlessness involves a physical dexterity that is the trademark of the seasoned, expert clown.

the lid and hollow metal poles telescope out magically to form a hanger for his costume changes. The lid itself is a mirror, and a round board clamped against it sprouts legs and becomes his stool. A top drawer swings up on hinges to lock into place under the mirror, and his makeup room is ready.

His costumes have been carefully packed in proper order for all the changes he must make; they will be hung up one by one after each act during the first show, ready for use during the second, after which, if the show moves on that night, they will go back into the trunk in their proper rotation.

A European trainer, the Great Blasjak, clowns with his favorite cat. Note how far back his hips and legs are, although he appears to be much closer to the lion. He can jerk his upper body back quickly enough but probably could not move his feet in time to avoid a quick (playful?) strike.

Order is everything to a circus and especially to a circus clown. The big shows move with a precision that the military has tried from time to time to emulate, mostly unsuccessfully. Each time a show sets up, the clown knows that his trunk will be in exactly the same place as it was the last time. The position is determined largely by seniority and never changes through the entire run. In the thirties and forties under canvas each clown could also expect two buckets of water to be set by his trunk, freshly filled once per day. One was his sudsing bucket and the other for rinsing. Soap and face cloth were retrieved, usually still damp, from a small tin container bolted in one corner of the trunk and the clown washed himself after each show. "You learned," one clown told me with a rueful smile, "not to spill your bucket. Any water you slopped over, you stood in for the rest of that run."

Today, of course, all the indoor arenas used by the circus have dressing rooms and showers, which makes a current clown union demand that circus trains be fitted with one shower per certain number of performers seem especially redundant. "Maybe their girl friends are insisting," suggested one exasperated circus official.

In the space-conscious circus the clown lived the full season out of that one trunk. He usually had two pairs of street trousers, two shirts, and three pairs each of underwear and socks, "One on me, one in the bucket, and one in the trunk," a veteran clown explained. He had no need for an elaborate personal wardrobe because he ate, talked, and slept circus—especially if he was in a three-high double. Producing clowns who manufactured the props used by the others had the luxury of extra prop boxes full of tools, string, nails, and wire from which they fashioned an incredible array of improvised gags. Other clowns made suggestions, helped out, or worked on new tricks and variations of their current routines.

No clown could change his routine or props without permission from the head clown, usually a senior member who dressed in his clown face and costume but spent most of his time under the big top unobtrusively supervising his fellows. Even a prop broken during a walk-around could be replaced by a different one only after it was ascertained that repair was impossible between shows. Timing was and is so important that the introduction of a new prop might throw off the show's movement. Clowning was a full-time job, with the major effort going on when the big top was dark; the dedication showed in the performance.

Clowns supply their own costumes except for the big finale spec which usually features oversize, feathered, and spangled get-ups owned and maintained by the circus. The new drip-dry fabrics have changed clowning by easing the performer's personal discomfort. In the old days of cotton tights when, as one clown recalls, it rained for 68 out of 75 days in New England, the clown would throw his tights into his wash bucket after the last show so they wouldn't mildew. They were fine, if somewhat uncomfortable, donned wet for the first show the next day, fitting very slickly, close to the skin. By the end of the matinee, however, the fabric had ballooned out from all the cavorting around, causing a severe case of *grapefruit knees* that would never snap back into shape for the next performance.

To avoid going on with sloppy-looking, baggy knees the clown would put a nickel down in his crotch, twist the cotton around until his knees came up tight, then tuck the twist under his athletic supporter. It usually held until near the end when the reemergence of the *grapefruits* was viewed by the crowd as simply another costume change.

The fifth and last row in the men's side of the dressing tent was populated by the cowboys and Indians. Like everything else in the circus there was a good reason for their being placed in that particular spot. They were right next to the outer canvas wall, a plus as long as it didn't rain. When it rained, water nearly always seeped in where tent wall and top joined, soaking paleface and redskin alike and getting their gear all wet. And that was why they were in the fifth row. Of all the costumes worn by the different performers theirs was the least susceptible to damage by water. Soaked blankets and buckskins would dry out; leather chaps and saddles were very nearly indestructible if dried properly. So the lowly clown, one step above the workingmen, won a reprieve from being in the last row because, as always, circus practicality overrode all other considerations.

Through the years a curious bond was established between the workingmen and the clowns. Segregated by the rigid circus caste system—the great mess tent had a *long* or workingmen side and a *short* or performer side separated by the luxury of a canvas wall—the clowns did not fraternize with the laboring crew. To have struck up a friendship with a typically illiterate, physically unclean razorback—the term comes from a crew bending double under a sideways-mounted wagon on a flatcar, then lifting on the command of "Raise your backs!" so that the wagon was turned wheels front to be rolled off—would have lowered a clown in the eyes of his peers. Workingmen had no personal belongings, because there was no place to keep any, and were not given water-bucket privileges. Food, shelter, and clothing were provided so they had little need of money, yet what to do with the princely sum of $3.50 per week paid in cash by the management?

In addition to being good daring fun this is interesting for what it's not: It's not a clown with a lion. Real clowns frighten big cats and only a trainer would dare put on this phony face for the sake of the show.

Some of the money would go for tobacco and booze; the remainder, if kept in a bunk car, would surely be stolen or, failing that, would be frivolously spent with no thought of tomorrow. Enter the clowns. The workingmen trusted the clowns who were nearest to their station in circus life and who usually were more mature than flyers or bareback riders. It was the rare clown who, at the season's start, was not approached by one or more workingman with the question, "Will you save money for me this year?" And the clown always did. Each week the razorback brought half of his $3.50 to the clown, who stashed it until the big top was dropped for the last time. Then he gave the accumulated savings to his "depositors," each man often realizing in excess of forty dollars, probably as much money as he had seen in a lump sum all of his life. The clowns never charged for this service and their honesty was legendary. The deal had only one proviso: if the workingman failed to come up with his weekly quota or asked for a draw on his poke, he got everything he had deposited back immediately and all further contact was terminated; the clowns were not ledger keepers and would brook no financial shilly-shallying.

All the hardships and personal discomfort vanish when the clowns step through the entrance into the circus arena. Whether it was under a six-pole big top that seated twelve thousand people, with the sunlight softly diffused through the white canvas, or in some modern hall such as Madison Square Garden or The Forum in Los Angeles, the feeling of pine shavings (one hundred bales of them) under foot and the up-tempo lead-in by the band offers the clown his moment of fulfillment. Out he comes, then and now, seemingly aimless, perpetually surprised, yet flawlessly repeating the same routine five times with apparent spontaneity during his two-minute start-and-stop journey around the track.

His timing had better be right else the thundering hooves of the equestrian acts making their entrance at a full gallop will overtake him or the "motley hordes" of elephants, chariots, and wagons of every description will send him running and stumbling, the crowd's appreciative laughter doing little to dim the ringmaster's scathing rebuke. But in the show, doing his routines, he is a master because, until recently, he had to be to survive.

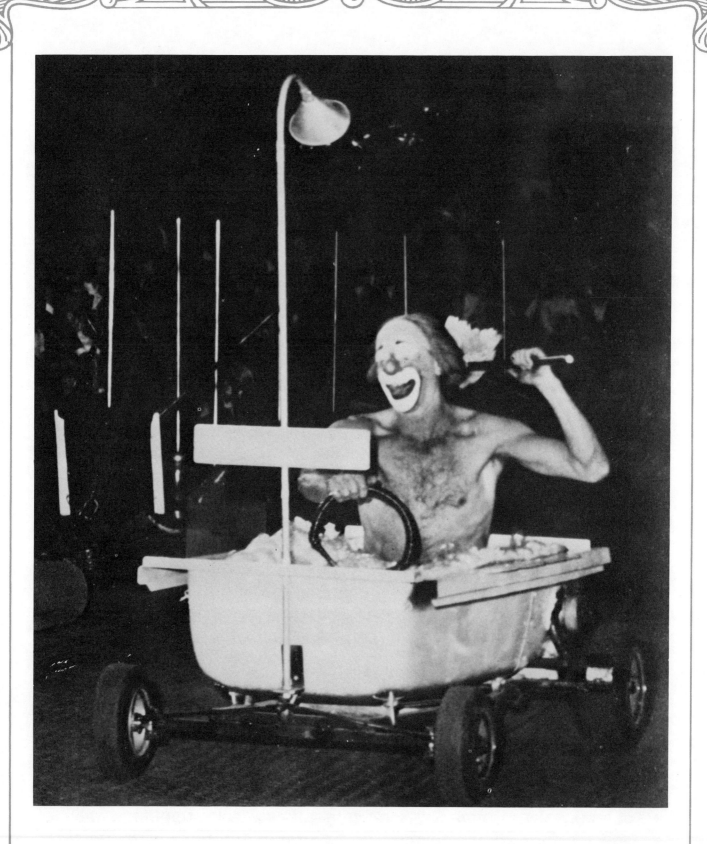

Lou Jacobs takes shaving on the way to work a couple of steps farther. Jacobs, a "producing" clown, thinks up and manufactures many of his own gags.

Watch him. He works *big* and, mostly, he works *high.* "When in doubt, make it bigger" is a basic tenet of all circus clown humor.

Two clowns stop during their walk-around; one brandishes a balloon and the other, with exaggerated gestures, urges him to blow it up. He does, pausing as it gets bigger and bigger, to hear his partner, now joined by the crowd, cheering him on. As the balloon gets improbably huge, the encouraging yells come from higher and higher in the seats as his partner reacts with uncertainty—he is working *high* and well, getting everyone involved. Finally, after an excruciating pause or two, his whole body appears to swell as he takes an enormous breath and blows; the balloon explodes in his face, he does a back somersault; to the roar of that section and his partner's obvious I-told-you-so gestures, he moves on to the next stop.

It is much easier for a clown to work *low*, worrying only about the first ten rows and ignoring the paying customers up out of his line of sight. Lazy clowns do this but, until the last seven or eight years, there were no lazy clowns in the circus. Not that working low is necessarily bad. Emmett Kelly worked low, picking out an attractive female member of the audience and, sitting in front of her, staring mournfully until her initial embarrassment turns to laughter echoed from the seats around her. But Kelly also worked *big.* Anyone who remembers how he employed an enormous mallet to crack a peanut shell, then reacted sadly when he crushed it flat will realize that he was practicing basic clown humor.

When he *thinks big* the clown is reflecting the very essence of the American circus itself. The first circuses were small, following the European tradition of family-owned-and-staffed shows. But it was impossible to spread out into the vast American hinterland and stay small. The size of the country demanded bigness, and the early circus owners were quick to oblige. Rather than a conscious economic act the enlargement of the circus began as a state of mind; the circus pushed farther south and west; the tents grew wider and longer, the rings more numerous and larger. Everything expanded and the clown, who first worked the carpet alone playing to two or three hundred people, had to change, too.

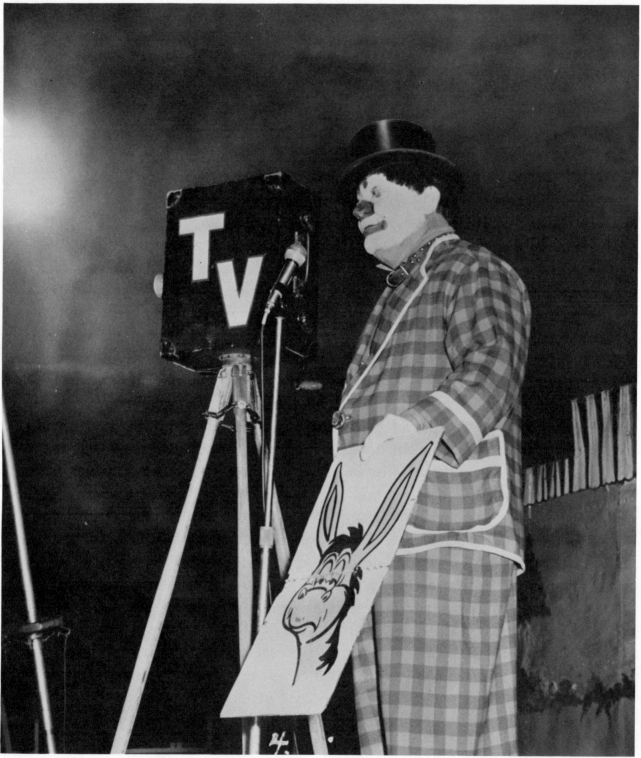

Keeping up with the times—or is he? Veteran Harry Ross hearkens back to the mid-nineteenth-century talking clowns by introducing politics into his act.

Harry Ross, a long-time clown, remembers some growing pains. "I remember being on a show that had a horse act, me, one elephant, and one camel," he recalled recently at the weekly Paul Eagles Circus Luncheon Club meeting in Philippe's restaurant in Los Angeles, where a section lined with circus memorabilia is traditionally set aside. "The owner had overextended himself and we were doing terrible business. Finally it got so bad that he could pay us for only two more nights and we'd have to close. The night of his announcement the camel died. That really did it. Everyone sat around staring, not saying anything, when suddenly this guy who put up billboards for us had an idea.

"The poster man hightailed it for our next stop and visited the local newspaper office. An event, he explained, unheard of in the annals of the circus had occurred and, although all the performers were severely shaken up, the show would go on as promised. The editor pressed him for details.

"It seemed that the elephant and the camel had gotten into a fight and the elephant had killed the dromedary in a fit of rage. 'Was the elephant safe to be around?' inquired the editor. 'Yes,' our man replied, 'but he could be viewed only under canvas, it was too risky to parade him outside in the usual manner.'"

Ross bit into one of Philippe's justly renowned French dip sandwiches and chewed ruminatively. "We sold out the next night and every night after that for the whole run. People didn't care about the show; they came to see the elephant that had killed the camel."

We began this little section with a Barnum quotation and we've closed it with Harry Ross's practical mud-show demonstration of the great showman's more famous "There's a sucker born every minute" maxim.

What makes people react to the circus, any circus, the way they do? This is a book on the American clown, not a psychological study; however, one aspect of audience reaction merits our inspection. Why do we laugh at *sad* clowns? Let's hear what clowns themselves and other experts have to say.

6
FUNNY OR SAD?

Oddly enough, one of this century's better known white-face "sad" clowns didn't spring from the circus at all. Harry Langdon, whom writer John Montgomery describes as "a small, pathetic white-faced clown who was nearly always on the verge of tears," is usually, in the public mind, a 1920s motion picture comedian. Mainly remembered for his work with Mack Sennett and as the star of some Chaplinesque comedies, Langdon actually worked a traveling medicine show as a clown prior to going to Hollywood.

He became a student of Chaplin and his techniques and realized one of his greatest successes when he teamed with Frank Capra, a young Sennett gag writer who would later become famous as director of *Mr. Deeds Goes to Town* and *It Happened One Night*, to write and star in *The Strong Man*. Langdon, as can be seen in the unusual photograph of him in this volume, fits our description of a classic, low-key clown.

The author had many long conversations with Mack Sennett (born Michael Sinnott in a small town in the province of Quebec, Canada) a year before he died, and he talked about Langdon in the old days. "Langdon started out as a prop man with a vaudeville troupe," the famous slapstick director recalled. "He was an Iowa boy bitten by the bug. He adored Chaplin. That's the way he was really, that hesitant, worried character he played on the screen." Sennett, an inveterate tobacco-chewer, expectorated in a graceful arc across his startled listener's outstretched legs and appeared not to notice the involuntary jump. "What most people didn't know was that Harry Langdon wanted to be a serious actor but was afraid to tell anybody—but me, I guess. But I wasn't making anything too serious in those days." Sennett gazed out of his window in the old Garden Court Apartments on Hollywood Boulevard. "He was a good comic. It was in him, you know. He could reach right out from that screen."

"It was in him." As it must be in every successful clown. But why did people laugh at his pathos? Bobby Kay, for more than forty years a top circus clown, whose face evolved into a modified-classical white with grotesque overtones, pondered that question in his com-

Harry Langdon, a slapstick star of the silent screen, in a lesser-known role.

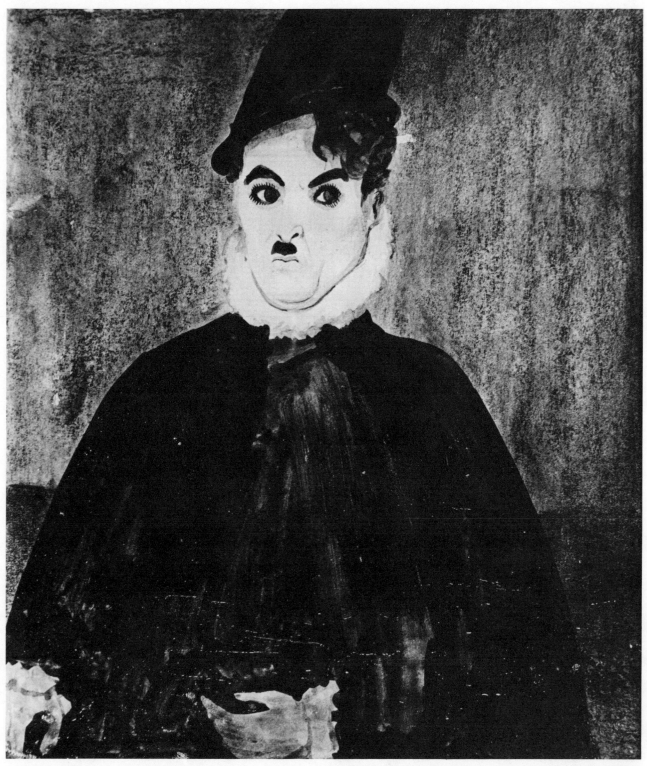

The little tramp in a pose by artist John Decker befitting the new dignity of Sir Charles Chaplin.

fortable Hollywood home where he lives, of course, in semi-retirement.

"I don't think that a clown's sad expression is what brings on laughter," Bobby suggested. "I think it's the shock of seeing this person who is supposed to be so happy, looking sad. I don't believe in the sad, Otto Griebling kind of clown. I never go around with a long puss. I have to work 'up' while other clowns prefer to work 'down.'"

Kay, who thinks Griebling a far superior clown to Emmett Kelly, remembers Griebling's attempts to convert him. "Otto was a dear, dear friend and one of the kindest men I ever knew. He would constantly make suggestions to me about facial expressions that I would try; but they were not for me. When Otto did them they were great but they looked terrible on me."

Griebling broke into the circus as a carpet clown about the time that Poodles Hanneford, one of the greatest riding clowns of all time, was at the height of his fame. In those days there were many times that the ring was wet or dangerously uneven, and the circus didn't want to risk Poodles, their greatest drawing card. Griebling was pressed into service and, wearing the same makeup—big fur coat, derby hat, and red wig—as the star, he would ride in his place without the audience knowing the difference. Griebling was a good rider to begin with and became as accomplished as Poodles over the years. They both rode in the tradition of the French Pierrots who were with the Astley Show in Paris and London at the beginning of the nineteenth century. Kochmanski, a European-trained riding clown who appears regularly in American circuses wearing a costume that strongly suggests the Chaplin influence, has carried on in the Pierrot-Hanneford-Griebling tradition.

Why laugh at a sad clown? Dr. Loriene Chase, a prominent clinical psychologist who specializes in meditation and dream analysis, considered her answer. "Clowns and clowning represent kind of a dream world to most of us," she told me. "We can feel comfortable with a clown when we see him looking sad because of some problem; we see ourselves in him and are able to laugh." The attractive authoress of *The Human Miracle* smiled. "That sad clown is us

*In the tradition of Poodles Hanneford, European riding star Kochmanski per-
forms in the center ring. He adopted a Chaplin-style face to help Americanize
his act.*

taking life much too seriously. We can see that he's making a big problem out of nothing and by laughing at him we are actually getting our own troubles into perspective. Lack of laughter is a deprivation of the spirit and the sad clown reminds us that we are depriving ourselves and that we had better get with it. We respond by laughing and enjoying ourselves."

Another reason we laugh at a mournful whiteface or tramp is the relief we feel because we know that he doesn't really mean his sadness. He is putting us, and by extension our supposed problems, on; the joke is on us and we permit ourselves the luxury of laughing at ourselves. How often have we seen an adult turn a child's temper tantrum into a hopeless giggle by mimicking the small, distorted face. That is what the clown does to us. "There you sit," he seems to be saying, "with the cares of the world on your poor tired shoulders. Nonsense!" And because it is nonsense and we have been caught taking ourselves too seriously, we laugh.

There is nothing as unfunny as a sad clown who doesn't make us laugh. We doubly resent him: first he is not amusing, and second he has made us feel embarrassment for him. He has ceased to be a clown and has exposed himself as a human being, an unforgivable effrontery. Usually when a sad clown fails to amuse it is because he confuses comedy and tragedy, a surprisingly easy thing to do if you try to work "low."

A modern example of this seeming inability to distinguish between humor and pathos is seen in popular comedian Jerry Lewis. Lewis, an outstanding slapstick performer who can be riotously funny when he is playing "up," has always missed the mark when he attempts to inject a note of pathos into his act. Coming off as neither amusing nor tragic he leaves the audience guessing as to his intentions, a fatal condition for a clown.

Heretical though it may seem, not everyone thinks that clowns, sad or otherwise, are funny. Maurice Gorham, in his book *Showmen and Suckers,* begins, "To speak against clowns verges on treason against the circus, which still pins its faith in them. . . . There are two main uses for clowns in the big, modern circus show— the regular number by the starred clowns and the recurrent incursions of the miscellaneous clowns who come on between the acts. It is of these last that I mean.

"To me it is a pathetic sight when an act finishes, the ring grooms rush in to remove its apparatus and set up for the next, and with them comes a horde of miscellaneous clowns in all varieties of grotesque makeup and with varied props, to keep the ring busy until the next turn is ready, when they are summarily called off. Sometimes their individual tricks are ingenious enough, but they have no real chance to make an impression with them. From the ringside seats the grotesque makeup seems to sober the children rather than amuse them, and from the top rows the only impression you get is that the ring is full of people all doing different things, which is presumably all the showman wants."

Without intending to, Mr. Gorham has made our case for the American clowns being unique performers as opposed to those of other countries; for the English author was writing about European clowns who, accustomed to small circuses, have never learned to work high and have, in fact, been often cast in the role of a carpet-clown chorus, there to distract rather than to be an integral part of the show. The European star-clowns like Grimaldi and Grock did not perform as part of a group—the first among equals—as do, say, Lou Jacobs and Mark Anthony today; they were often *the* star attraction of the entire circus and as such were considered to be not only far above the common variety of clowns but also in a different category altogether. They worked alone, as featured performers.

What happens today when a star from another field of entertainment becomes a clown? I decided to ask one who, in the public mind, is not generally associated with clowning. Ernest Borgnine invited me to his Beverly Hills home where we talked about a little-known side of the Academy Award-winning actor.

"I've been interested in clowns and clowning for a long time," he began, "but I really got involved because of an appearance on "The Johnny Carson Show." Johnny and I were talking and he said, 'Ernie, you've done just about everything in show business. Is there anything left that you'd like to do?'

"I said there was; I'd like to be a clown.

Australian clown Harold Simmons was encouraged by Mark Anthony to try his luck in the United States and was greatly influenced by the American tramp.

Mark Anthony at an early stage of his career before he settled into his tramp face and ragged costume.

Producing-clown Mark Anthony tuning up for the circus band.

"Johnny laughed and warned me, 'You'll get some letters,' and sure enough I did. The one that intrigued me most was from the Joseph Schlitz Brewing Company in Milwaukee. They sponsor a huge Fourth-of-July parade there every year and they said that if I really wanted to be a clown they would feature me in their parade the next year."

The actor smiled broadly in what, depending on your generation, you might take as the menacing leer of Fatso in *From Here to Eternity,* the good-natured grin of Marty, or the frustrated grimace of Lieutenant-Commander McHale in television's "McHale's Navy." Actually the actor is a well-spoken, gracious man with a finely honed sense of humor, a Marty who improbably lives in a hilltop mansion and uses a Cadillac rather than the subway as his means of transportation.

"I made my first public appearance as a clown in Milwaukee in 1970," Borgnine recalled. "And it was a real thrill. I had the time of my life."

The actor discussed his clown face. "We didn't try to take away the likeness of Borgnine the actor," he explained. "We wanted to give the impression of a clown but not lose the other identity. And we had a very good reason. So many of the kids, and grown-ups too, recognized me as McHale from "McHale's Navy" and the combination of McHale and the clown really made a big hit."

How did he feel the first time he looked into a mirror and saw himself as a full-fledged clown?

"An amazing thing happened," the actor remembers. "As the fellow began putting on my makeup, I felt just a little apprehensive, even solemn. After all, this was not like being made up for the cameras; someone was putting lines and color on my face that I had really no knowledge of. I asked for a mirror to check the progress. I didn't say anything, but solemn was the word for what I saw.

"Then suddenly, it all seemed to come together. Something blossomed inside of me as I sat up and looked into the big dressing-table mirror. It was an almost spiritual feeling. There I was, Ernie Borgnine but not quite Ernie Borgnine. I was someone else, too, and I liked what I saw and felt. I was a clown and knew how a clown should act just as though I had been working as one for years."

A basic actor's instinct?

"Partly. But I think it was a long-held-back desire suddenly being let free. It was a wonderful feeling. It was so strong that if I believed in reincarnation I would say that I was a clown in some previous life and that it carried over. I don't know."

The face that evolved is that of a carpet clown, human and not too far out, in the tradition of Griebling and Kelly.

"It was an entirely new experience for me," the star continued. "I found that, in spite of the simple makeup, I felt that I could hide behind that face. The probing camera was gone and I could understand how a clown could perform without having to let people know how he really felt."

I asked him why a man who was at the peak of his profession should decide to tell Johnny Carson and millions of viewers that he wanted to be a clown. What made him do it?

"It goes back a long way," he told me. "My mother instilled a love of opera in me and I remember even as a youngster thinking how great it was that in *Pagliacci* the clown performed even though his heart was breaking. I think that the idea of a clown being able to entertain despite his sadness, the idea that he can shut himself off and perform, has always appealed to me. Now that I've done it myself—not that I had a great sadness to hide or anything like that—but now that I've worn a face I can understand the meaning of *Pagliacci* even more."

I asked him if he enjoyed any particular type of clown.

"Well, I worked with Lou Jacobs in one of the circus parades." Borgnine smiled at the recollection. "We were both riding on top of a wagon doing little bits, waving to the kids, that kind of thing. One of us said, 'Let's work up a little routine,' and we did, right on the spot, and used it all the way through the parade. I don't even remember what it was now, but I'll never forget the thrill of working with Jacobs. He's one of the best.

"Basically, though, I'd like a chance to give my own interpretation of a clown either in a motion picture or on the stage. One of my favorite stories is "The Day the Clown Cried"; it's about someone who led a group of children to their deaths in the so-called baths in one of the concentration camps. A story like that, I think, would

be a real challenge to any actor. I understand that Jerry Lewis filmed it in Europe but that it has never been released over here."

I asked the actor his thoughts on why a sad clown would make people laugh.

"I can't answer that," he said. "Unless it's because they don't actually believe the clown. I know that I have never played it that way but I have realized that I'm behind some kind of façade even though the face is still Borgnine. I don't think I'd even want to play it sad for the simple reason that I'm enjoying myself too much. I let all my inhibitions come out and do things that seem to me at the time to be a little foolish; but no matter what I do, people laugh and that makes me very happy."

More so than a good screen performance?

"Well, there's a directness about it; people respond and any actor will tell you that when you hear that live applause or laughter it's a great feeling and makes you really take off.

"You'd be surprised how good it feels to be a clown," Borgnine continued. "It's kind of like therapy after the discipline of working in front of a camera."

I talked about some of those great on-camera performances, especially the great heavies he used to play. There were times, I recalled, when he had me so angry with him that I wanted to get up and personally retaliate for something he had just done to the hero.

Borgnine roared with laughter. "Me too," he said.

I asked if he could be that objective.

"Oh, very much so," he replied. "I can watch myself and always learn something. Now that I think about it, I do believe that I like clowning so much because of all those sinister roles. I think I want people to see me and say, 'Hey, that Ernie Borgnine isn't such a bad guy after all.'

"Ideally I think an actor should be able to turn it on and off when he's working. To me that's what professionalism really means. You go on the set, the action starts, you act, the action stops, and you become your real self. I've worked with some people who, if they have to go into a scene panting, say, will hold up the action

while they run around the sound stage until they get the proper mood. Then, when the scene is over, they keep in character. They forget that they have to live with their fellow man. They think that they can live constantly in a make-believe world created by authors. It gets ridiculous after a while."

Would he like to work in a circus?

"Love to, if I had the time. I've been invited to appear when the circus is playing here on the West Coast but my work involves a lot of traveling and we've just never come together."

The star, in his clown role, visits children's hospitals whenever his schedule permits, and these unpublicized appearances give him a great deal of pleasure.

"I remember one time," he said, "I was in the children's ward of a big hospital and I had been going from bed to bed talking to the kids and everyone was having a good time. I had spotted this little redheaded boy in a bed set away from the others at the far end of the room. He was obviously in pain but he was watching me all the time. When I finally got to him he was a little shy at first, but soon we were talking and he managed a smile; I got really caught up in our conversation. Suddenly, right in mid-sentence, he turned his little face up to me and said, 'I think you better go now. You see, it hurts a lot and I don't want to cry in front of you.' "

One of the screen's greatest tough guys looked at the interviewer, started to say something, stopped, then, after a deep breath, laughed apologetically. "I guess that's what being a clown really means to me," he said.

7
BASIC
TYPES

There are three basic types of clown makeup.

The first is the classical whiteface used by George L. Fox and Harry Langdon and, more recently, by Pat Valdo, Harold Hall, and Harry Dann.

The second is the auguste (pronounced oh-goost) baggy-pants clown with exaggerated makeup and clothing and best exemplified by Lou Jacobs.

The third is what originally was called the carpet clown but, with the term broadened now to include the auguste, is generally recognized as the tramp character clown made famous by Griebling and Kelly. Strictly speaking, however, the tramp or character clown is the original carpet clown and remains, as we have explained elsewhere, probably the one truly indigenous American clown.

All manner of variations have sprung from these three basic types. We have already dealt with the origins of the carpet clown. The whiteface subdivides into "neat" and "grotesque." The neat whiteface is perhaps the purest form in that it features small markings around the eyes, a modest mouth, a skullcap, and a tiny hat perched atop a hairless head. The shoes are very light, thin pumps that reflect the European origin of the makeup. In the sixteenth century the clown or Harlequin wore a *socci,* heelless, light shoes that kept him as small as possible so as not to obstruct the audience's view of the principal dramatic actors who worked upstage behind him and wore buskins, high thick-soled boots that made them more visible down front.

The grotesque whiteface uses the same reds and blacks as the neat but applied much more boldly so that the mouth becomes a large splash of color, hair sprouts on both sides of the head, eyebrows become thick black slashes, and the nose often puffs out into a large bulb. The thin, ballet-style shoes give way to enormous, splayed feet either human or animal; the general impression is of a much broader comedic approach that lends itself to working high.

Both neat and grotesque wear similar loose-fitting costumes covered with colorful patches or spangles. These traditional clown costumes are said to have originated in mid-seventeenth-century France when the famous playwright Molière, casting a play and

Pat Valdo, a neat whiteface clown who worked in the middle thirties for Ringling Bros.

looking for a simpleton type, dressed a clown character in the voluminous smock of the French peasant.

The auguste clown, the fellow with the tremendously exaggerated face whose clothes don't fit him and who is the slapstick specialist, makes us laugh just looking at him. Lou Jacobs has brought the auguste act to the status of fine art. The costume's origins, according to French writer Georges Strehly in *L'Acrobatie et les Acrobats,* can be traced to the 1860s, when an unknown clown appeared in an oversized, ill-matched set of formal tails doing a drunk act. M. Willson Disher, however, claims that a German-born American clown named Tom Belling became the first auguste in Berlin quite by accident. Belling, dressed in the tailored finery of a ringmaster, stumbled while entering the ring and, to cover his clumsiness, went into a drunk act. The crowd yelled "August," in encouragement. The next day he changed into some cast-off clothes several sizes too large for him and became an auguste clown.

We can only assume that the term "August"—a first name—was used as a colloquialism similar to the American "do a Brodie" from that same period, a coinage meaning, "to take a fall," after the exploits of Steve Brodie, a New York newsboy who claimed to have jumped off the Brooklyn Bridge.

According to an anonymous European etymologist the circus usage stems from a Viennese clown who achieved such popularity that his first name worked its way into the language as a metonym for "silly." The crowd yelling *"Der dumme August"* at the performer soon became any audience wanting to express itself and forgoing the *dumme* for the simple *"August,"* with the original meaning intact. The word itself can be traced to the mid-sixteenth century, probably of Low German origin, when it meant a peasant or a clod.

Whatever its origin the, to the English-speaker's ear, awkward, inappropriate expression stuck fast to one of the funniest of the performing clowns. Many of the traditional clown gags rely for their execution on the auguste clown. His makeup tends to have a more pinkish base than the whiteface, and he relies heavily on props that he has frequently devised himself.

SELLS & GRAY CIRCUS

Whiteface clowns always say "Circus." These examples of neat and grotesque whites promise fun without infringing on any specific clown face. The firecracker calls to mind all the great gag explosions from the House on Fire to the Exploding Car that we look forward to seeing again.

The tramp, uniquely an American face,
began as a carpet clown charged with all manner of circus duties.
His makeup generally retains a human identity
and his clothes are designed to withstand a knockabout existence.

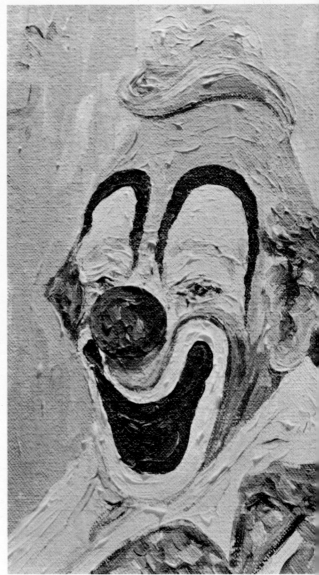

The three basic clown types shown here are: Auguste, Lou Jacobs (above right); Whiteface, Harry Dann (above left); Tramp—Carpet, Emmett Kelly (right). Original paintings by Dyer Reynolds

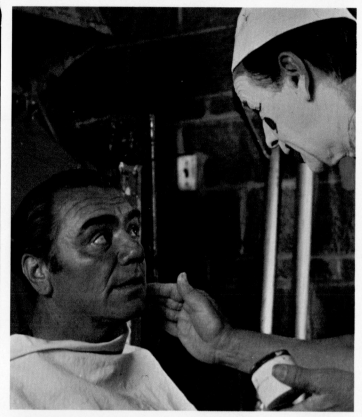

Ernest Borgnine's transformation from motion picture star to clown is more than skin deep. He discusses his emotions in an interview with the author.

On this page we see the clown star of the annual Schlitz Fourth-of-July parade in Milwaukee demonstrating both his versatility and his obvious gusto.

The new breed of female clowns
display their femininity in the best tradition of women's equality:
but are they in the best clown tradition?
Here are two whiteface ladies with grotesque overtones.
The costumes emphasize beauty rather than buffoonery.

Below, clockwise from the rabbit: Frankie, Mike, Frosty, and Bobby entertain at the White House in 1970. Clowns are apolitical professionally, which may account for their infectious good spirits. Note the similarity between neat whitefaces veteran Harold Hall (left), and ex-sailor Frosty, in photographs taken forty years apart.

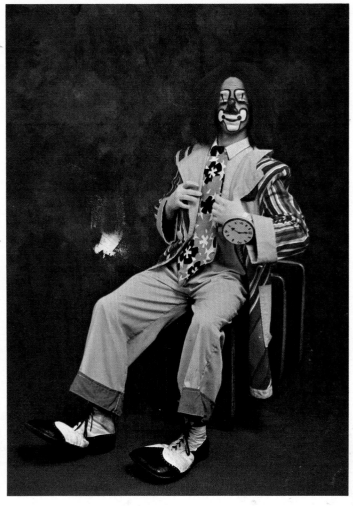

Laugh, clown, laugh
is really what it's all about.
These four grotesque-auguste artists
invite our answering smiles.

Once again, the neat whiteface tells the whole story. P.T. Barnum's advice that "Clowns and elephants are the two pegs that you hang the circus on" is taken to heart in this 1972 version of an early circus lithograph used by the Big John Strong Show.

Far right: An auguste clown performs the traditional carpet function of pointing the way to the coming action in this unusually stylized lithograph. Perhaps the featured "escapees" contribute to the melodramatic tone of this Bartok one-sheet, as the standard size litho is called.

CIRCUS

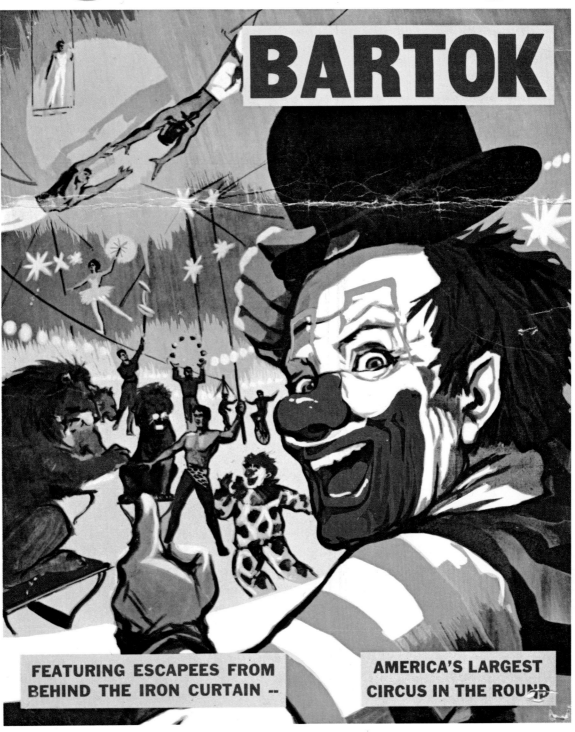

BARTOK

FEATURING ESCAPEES FROM
BEHIND THE IRON CURTAIN --

AMERICA'S LARGEST
CIRCUS IN THE ROUND

CLYDE BEATTY-COLE BROS. CIRCUS

THE WORLD'S LARGEST CIRCUS

RINGLING BROS WORLD'S GREATEST SHOWS

ARMY OF 50 CLOWNS

Above left: This Clyde Beatty—Cole Bros. clown poster ballyhoos the arrival of the "World's Largest Circus." "The Greatest Show on Earth" might disagree, but the day is long passed when rival shows tore down one another's "paper" and replaced it with their own. As many as fifty poster men preceded a show to blanket the next stop with their wares.

Above: Nothing but clowns are needed to advertise the coming of the Hagen Bros. Circus in the 1950s. Neat white, grotesque, and the suggestion of auguste faces make a bold, happy lithograph, the accepted name for all circus posters no matter what reproduction technique is employed.

Left: A turn-of-the-century clown poster reprinted shortly before 1919 when Ringling Brothers formally combined with Barnum and Bailey. Although the pictured ethnic clowns have vanished, the whitefaces in the lower left and right corners have changed little in more than fifty years.

—Circus World Museum

The Barnum & Bailey Greate

VERITABLE PANDÈMONIUM DE DRÔLERIES ACCOMPLIES PAR QUANTITÉ DES
AVANTURES ET MÉSAVENTURES LES PLUS COMIQUES ET LES PLUS RISIBI

RANDS COMIQUES DU MONDE, LES ÉPISODES
R LES PLUS ADROITS CLOWNS DU MONDE.

The clown band, once a circus staple, pictured in this 1898 poster announcing the original Greatest Show on Earth to a foreign audience. The severe whitefaces, the costuming, and the clown cricket match in the background reflect the European influence.

—Jos. Schlitz
Brewing Company

Right: Young clowns bring new ideas for makeup and costumes. The baggy-pants auguste breaks with tradition by "showing skin," taboo among veteran performers. The whiteface's costume suggests a modern version of the early rustic, popular in the 1920s and 1930s.

Below right: Not too long ago only wives or relatives of male clowns became clowns themselves and usually disguised their femininity. Now girl clowns are not only accepted but can work with men as a team.

Below: Popular entertainer Steve Allen receiving the Norman Carroll Memorial Award from a clown panel for "bringing one of the greatest gifts of all to millions of people all over the world—the gift of laughter." The award was established for Carroll, a former Big Top clown who became a celebrated ringmaster. Later, with his wife Shirley, he publicized the circus for many years.

—Norman Carroll Collection

This page: As the clown is to circus so the midget is to clowning. Starting out as a sideshow curiosity the midget has now become a full-fledged clown partner and a necessary part of many gag routines.

Opposite page: The whiteface, neat and grotesque versions pictured here, links the roving players of sixteenth-century Italy and the modern-day clown. More than any other, the whiteface means circus and, to most of us, circus means clown.

Official Program

35¢

3 RINGS 42 ACTS

AMERICA'S CLEANEST and Finest Entertainment

PERMANENT ADDRESS
ROUTE No. 2 – WILLARD, MISSOURI 65781
PHONE AREA CODE 417-862-6964

PROGRAM · FEATURES
PHOTOS · STORIES · COMICS
TWENTY FIVE CENTS

A program may or may not be a "magazine" but a sure way to sell it is to feature a clown on the cover. Here, a wide range of designs spans many decades and at least one ocean.

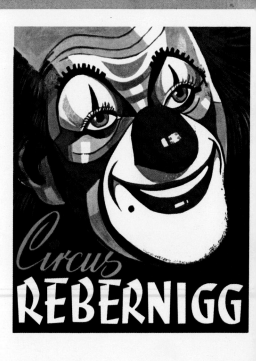

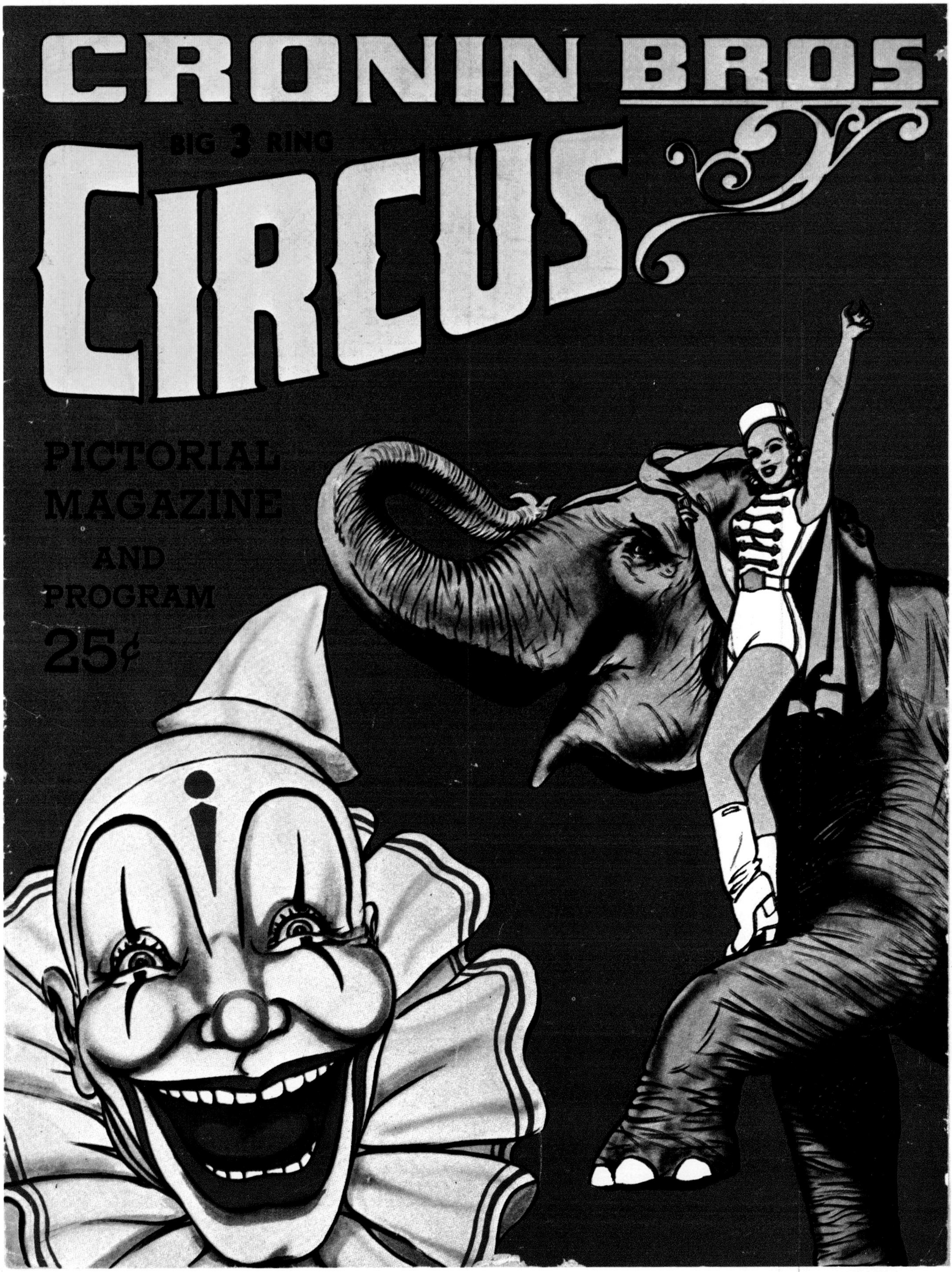

CRONIN BROS

BIG 3 RING

CIRCUS

PICTORIAL
MAGAZINE
AND
PROGRAM
25¢

The old and the new. The postage stamp includes parts of every traditional basic form of clown face. The younger clowns not only "show skin" but generally shy away from classic clown face and costume.

The three basic clown types gave birth to the Funny Rustic, the Motley Fool, the Musical Clown, the Bumpkin, the Sunny Jim, the Elegant, the Tumbler, the Fat-Boy, the Double Face, the Character (really a merging of the tramp and the auguste), the Riding Clown, and many others that even the oldest living circus people are hard put to identify. The reason for the proliferation was two-fold. First, as in so many things connected with the circus, economics shaped the art form. Many smaller circuses simply couldn't afford the purity of the basic types.

A neat whiteface, bowing to demands for versatility from a financially harassed mud-show operator, sprouted hair, a more flagrant face, and big shoes to edge toward his auguste cousin. The auguste in turn stayed on longer and longer until, in addition to his own routines, he fulfilled the carpet function of time-killing between acts. Since it was impractical to change makeup for every appearance, the small-circus clown gradually developed a face that would give him the best of all worlds. He would attempt to combine the "pure circus" of the whiteface, the exaggerated humor of the auguste, and the practicality of the carpet-tramp into one all-purpose performer who could work a two-ring show from start to finish by simply changing his costume and props.

Mark Anthony is an outstanding present-day example of that kind of adaptability. The big circus star has managed to combine auguste and carpet so that while he can work low to the first ten rows with some great sight gags that he has created, he also projects high to make more distant fans feel a part of the picture. Anthony is a producing clown, which means that he thinks up and makes with his own hands props for gags used both by himself and other clowns. One of his best-known routines—seen at one time or another by almost every circus-goer—is the watermelon gag, created by himself. It illustrates his ability to reach everyone in the circus audience.

He appears carrying a huge watermelon. He's happy carrying the watermelon, letting us know before he is five steps onto the track that this watermelon is the nicest thing that's happened to him in a long time. He also lets us know that he is going to eat that watermelon. So, in one of his six programmed performances during

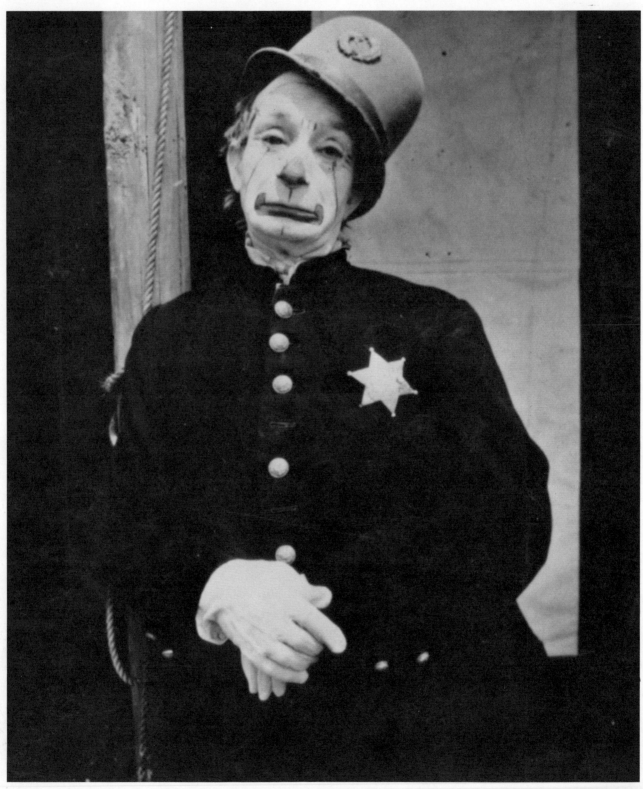

Abe Goldstein in his celebrated characterization as a Keystone Kop.

his walk-around, he stops, contemplates the melon, looks to the crowd for approval, then takes a bite. A stream of water hits him in the face; dismayed, he sorrowfully acknowledges the audience's laughter. And off he goes, followed by hundreds of hopeful stares until the clown behind him catches their attention and he has found a new section.

Anthony has two syringes inside the melon, each with a water-filled rubber bulb, just under either hand, a sufficient supply to last him around the arena. The gag is really a variation of the fire-hose routine used when the fire truck comes tearing out to rescue the baby from the burning house. While the "mother and child" howl plaintively from the smoke-filled second story, two firemen rush to hitch up the hose. Water is frantically turned on, the nozzle aimed, and a large stream squirts backward to drench the hapless firemen and delay the rescue.

Water has long been employed as a comic device, the use of a concealed syringe going back to the *commedia dell'arte* in seventeenth-century Italy when a freshly harvested grape unexpectedly squirted its would-be consumer in the face.

And so has smoke and "fire." Traditionally the conflagration involving the burning house or the exploding car has been provided by a lycopodium pot, consisting of a plain enamel pot fitted with a cover and containing a quantity of lycopodium powder. Lycopodium's characteristics are such that, when suddenly exposed to air, it gives off a fearsome-looking belch of flame and smoke that is immediately self-extinguished. Hence the cover. Enough gas must be generated inside the airless pot to provide each desired "explosion" but no harm is done because the air itself extinguishes the flash. Modern science has been unable to improve on the lycopodium pot as a practically risk-free producer of much circus fun.

Perhaps in this discussion of basic clown types and their offshoots we can put to rest once and for all the definition of what makes a clown. To paraphrase Dr. Johnson, "Sir, we *know* when we see a clown and *there's* an end on't." Very simply, a clown looks like a clown no matter what type he happens to be. In this sense Dan Rice was not a clown as Will Rogers was not, as Bob Hope is not.

All three men are remarkably alike in their power to entertain. It is as though one of their type must sprout every three or four generations. Each represents the quintessential American of his time. Each uses daily gossip as a basis for humorous political comment. Each stands alongside—or above—the President himself as representing the United States in the minds and hearts of both its own citizens and those of many foreign countries. Rice, Rogers, and Hope merit collective study as the embodiments of a continuing American phenomenon, but for our purposes it is what they are not, that is, clowns, that makes our point and isolates our definition.

No clown face can be copyrighted, but a face, once established, is seldom stolen outright, although various components—a teardrop here, an eyebrow there—are incorporated into other faces. The reason for this is as much practical as it is moral.

A clown face is hard to come by; it is the result of years of trial and error, of suggestions from fellow clowns, of observed reaction from audiences. Once it is set, it not only serves as a mark of identity but it conforms to the facial structure so that it looks natural in the sense that it doesn't intrude itself on the clown's normal features. A professional clown's face changes constantly during the early years of his development, sometimes not becoming definitely established until relatively late in his career. As the accompanying series of photographs shows, Bobby Kay (whiteface with grotesque overtones) went through some significant revisions in his face and costume before settling on the combination that has, for many years, made him a top circus clown.

"My makeup has evolved over forty years," Bobby told me. "Most clowns put on too much makeup at first; their face becomes too busy. Of course, as the years go by, all those wiggly-worms you were adding become natural and you have to start smoothing them out with greasepaint.

"In the old days when you were starting out other clowns would help you. They'd look at your face and tell you that your eyes are wrong, or your nose is crooked or your mouth isn't right. Suddenly, one day you make up and no one says anything to you; you know you've arrived and that your face is as near-perfect as it will ever be.

Bobby Kay in his first clown face appearing in the Chase & Son Circus, "A little turkey out of Colorado," in 1937.

With the Young Nelsons (lower right) on the Cole Brothers show in 1941.

Bobby Kay's first modern face in 1948.

Here he is again, an established star in 1965 with The Greatest Show on Earth.
The face looks the same, but there are a number of important, subtle differences.

"In my own case, as you can see in these pictures, with time the bags under my eyes got baggier; I moved those two little red teardrops away from the eye corners where they used to be, down to my cheekbones to shift attention away from the bags."

Kay, who teaches makeup to aspiring clowns now that he is semi-retired, continued. "And those two little marks on my forehead; they went on during an oriental period when those little yin and yang marks seemed to be the thing to do. I slowly enlarged them into big spots but gradually kept reducing them until they're back where they started thirty years ago. The only other thing I've changed is my eyebrows. I admired Mark Anthony's so much that I fixed myself up with a variation of his.

"Basically," the veteran clown said, "in thinking about the type of face I wanted I felt that I had to come through as a person, as something else than a mask. I don't want to be recognized on the street without my face yet I don't want to be scary with it; I might have a 'woeful countenance' but never a frightening one. I always wanted to greet people with a pleasant smile. That smile, incidentally, is something of an illusion in itself. It looks as though I have one of those big watermelon mouths when I smile, but I really do not. Those two little 'commas' on my cheeks join with my mouth in a smile that looks much broader than it is. A big painted mouth limits your expression. By using the illusion to produce the big smile I humanize myself and relate more closely to my audience."

And, like so many other facets of our society, television has brought changes to a clown's face.

"Television needs a very expressive face," Kay explained. "In the circus, as long as the face projects up into the audience the makeup is successful. When I do television, I give myself five to ten minutes extra makeup time to make sure that the lines are sharp and the colors right. I use a different white for TV. The chalk white that is so good in the circus will throw a halo around your face on the tube. So I pink my white—the way an auguste does all the time—just enough so that it shows up as true white on camera."

Clown makeup was quite possibly first used in its modern sense by the English clown Joseph Grimaldi as the result of a rather

Bobby Kay (left) is pleased with artist Dyer Reynolds's portrait of him in face and costume.

interesting set of circumstances. Grimaldi was appearing on the London stage in 1799 as Punch at Drury Lane. It began as a limited run, but such was its popularity that Grimaldi found himself playing the role well into its second year and that, as described by London *Star* drama critic A. E. Wilson, gave him problems.

"Punch's trappings were so heavy and cumbersome," Wilson wrote, "that they were more than Grimaldi could bear during the whole of the performance. He had to wear a large and heavy lump on his chest and back, a high sugar-loaf hat, a long-nosed mask, and heavy wooden shoes, the weight of the whole dress being enormous. He was compelled by fatigue and by the exertions of having to perform a great amount of comic business to assume Clown's dress at the end of the sixth scene."

And for the seventh scene Grimaldi put makeup on his face, not, apparently, because he thought it was an especially great idea, but because it supplied an illusion that he didn't have to carry around. According to Wilson, "This was the first occasion on which the Clown had appeared in full grotesque glory."

Bobby as he looks today, "semi-retired."

THE
MAN BEHIND
THE FACE

What is a clown really like? If there is such a thing as a typical clown in the sense of someone who has mastered his profession and is accepted as being one of the top performers in the business, then Bobby Kay must surely be able to answer our question. Now in his sixties, Bobby is as fit and spry as a whiteface half his age; he is a gentleman who also happens to be a gentle man, a most pleasing combination.

Robert Kay Smiley was born with that prophetic last name in Lewistown, Pennsylvania, in 1908. His mother was a concert pianist and his father a medical doctor "who made house calls." Bobby, his three brothers and one sister, and his mother and father formed a close-knit family unit all of whose members were encouraged to speak their minds on anything from the latest report card to their feelings about religion.

"We would gear our whole life pattern to being together for the evening meal," Bobby told me as we sat on the patio at his Hollywood home under the California winter sun. "Sometimes, because Dad was out making calls—a country doctor did that in those days—that meal wouldn't occur until 11 P.M." Neighbors and friends dubbed them "the late Smileys," and Bobby set his personal circadian clock to a cycle that he has kept ever since. He stayed in high school five years because, after the late-night family rap sessions, he could never make the first morning period. His circus life continued in the same work-late sleep-late vein and he doesn't regret his extra year in school.

"Dad was an agnostic and no joiner," Bobby remembers, "and I learned a lot from him. I'm still like him in some ways. I subscribe to the golden rule and feel as at home in a synagogue as in a Roman Catholic church."

Dr. Smiley, the name is derived from smilax, a plant with small, greenish, heart-shaped flowers indigenous to Scotland, where the family originated, wanted Bobby to go into medicine, but from the very beginning the boy's heart was in show business. When his pre-med first year at Syracuse University ended with more acting than academic credits, his father gave up on his son's medical career and Bobby went with the Jane Hastings Stock Company and ap-

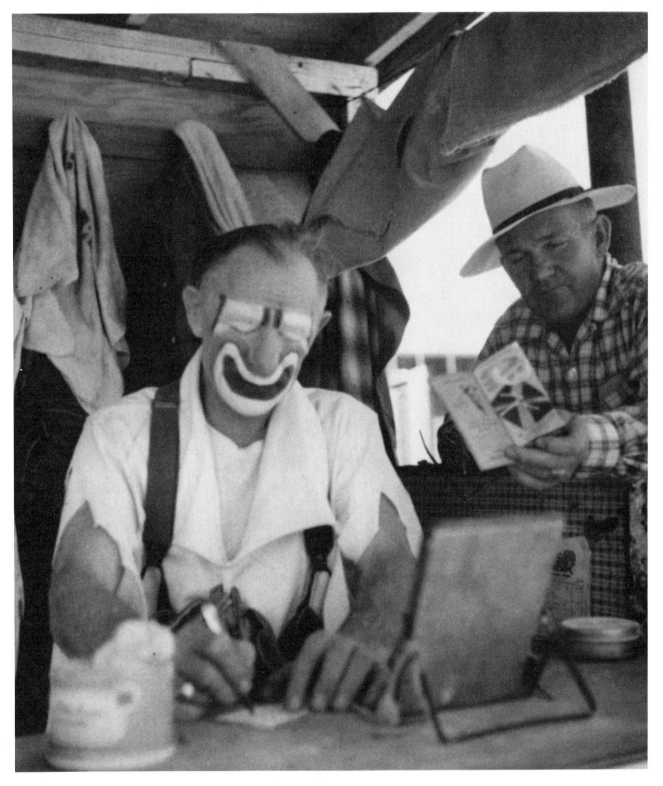

Lou Jacobs in an informal moment. Half human being, half clown.

1 Paul Wenzel
2 Owen (Duffy) McQuade
3 Mark Anthony
4 Glen (Kinko) Sunbury
5 Gene Lewis
6 Kochmanski
7 Irma Meadows
8 Dennis Stevens
9 Billy Ward
10 Laslo Donnertz
11 Otto Griebling
12 Marcos Droguett
13 Lou Jacobs
14 Prince Paul
15 Frankie Saluto
16 Jackie Cooper

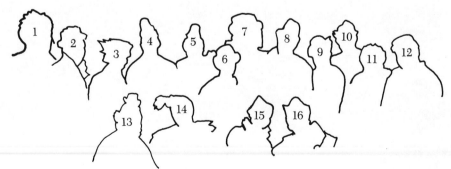

peared on the stage at the Temple Theatre in Lewistown. He was soon back in Syracuse, where he worked in vaudeville as a singer and dancer in addition to doing everything from scene painting to makeup. He took the big step of joining the Downey Brothers circus "with a clown suit and no knowledge" in 1923.

It was a difficult decision because the circus paid apprentice clowns two dollars a week plus their keep, and his family, especially his father, could not quite see the practicality of the move. Strangely enough, this phase of his clowning career was short-lived. An acrobatic act, billed as The Young Nelsons, playing with the circus needed an extra member and Bobby, naturally agile and with good balance, decided to accept their invitation.

That was a second big step for a young man just embarking on a circus career, because joining an act like the Nelsons involved practicing eight or nine hours a day in addition to doing the regular shows. The pay was better, though, because the Nelsons got a contract with the Paul Lewis circus in Jackson, Michigan, that paid Bobby fifteen dollars per week, from which three was deducted for a place to sleep in a wagon. Bobby smiles as he talks about the Nelsons.

"The original name of the act was Hodges, an Irish family who intermarried with the Hannefords of Poodles riding-clown fame. Circus names are like circuses themselves; they come and go like gypsies, blending in with the current trends, doing their thing, then moving on. Way back in the last century everyone felt that the only good performers were the Italians, because that is where a lot of the old circus families came from.

"So Hodges changed his name to Hodgini and toured the Continent, ending up in England at about the time that the English circus was coming into its own. Irishmen weren't too popular in England then, so Hodges-Hodgini became Hobson, a very respectable English name. Well, the Hobsons played for a while but, when they decided to come to the United States, they felt they needed a little extra push. Most Americans knew about Lord Nelson's victory at the battle of Trafalgar so Hodges-Hodgini-Hobson became The Young Nelsons. By the time I joined the act there wasn't an original Nelson in the crowd.

"But we did well," Bobby, a small, compactly built man, reminisced, "and had a great act with the Cole Brothers Circus in 1941. We did a Risley act, named after Walter Risley, an Australian who pioneered it over here. You know, where one man lies on his back with his legs up and supports the rest of the troupe in a pyramid on the soles of his feet. I was bottom man, the understander, and I guess I have that early leg development to thank for the fact that I still get around pretty good today."

The Second World War took one of the act and, try as they might, the Nelsons failed to replace the missing member. "We looked for a year," Bobby recalls. "And although we had some acrobats try out who were really better than any of us, we couldn't get the same rhythm going. We had learned to breathe together with very, very good timing and finally, when we realized that we just couldn't make it, we broke up.

"There was more to that Risley act than met the eye. As any acrobatic performer will tell you, the first thing he becomes aware of is the force of gravity. Nowadays, when the circus plays indoors and floors have been laid out level, gravity isn't such a big problem but in the days of the tent shows no patch of ground was truly flat. If you were lucky the drop-off may only have been one foot in a tent a hundred feet across but that was plenty. Lying on your back with your head and shoulders in line with the ground you had to create a new horizontal, using only experience and a natural sense of balance. In any pyramid the understander had to learn to make a short leg to compensate for the ground slope. It wasn't quite as easy as it looked.

"That's why so many flyers—the trapeze artists—are doing triple somersaults today when it was a rare event under the big top. The whole show stopped for the triple—and with good reason—although the audience probably didn't fully understand what they were seeing. The aerial rigging had to be absolutely vertical to the ground because a flyer loses all orientation going into the triple; everything becomes a blur. You're exerting seventeen hundred foot-pounds of pressure and, although you don't actually lose consciousness, you have no awareness of what is happening around you.

1 Laslo Donnertz
2 Gene Lewis
3 Mark Anthony
4 Paul Wenzel
5 Dennis Stevens
6 Owen McQuade
7 Billy Ward
8 Lou Jacobs
9 Kochmanski
10 Glen Sunbury
11 Otto Griebling
12 Frankie Saluto
13 Marcos Droguett
14 Irma Meadows
15 Prince Paul
16 Jackie Cooper

Harold Hall, a neat whiteface, Bobby Kay's partner for many years.

"You stay in your 'tuck' (rolled up in a ball to reduce wind resistance) until the catcher yells 'Break.' Then you have to instantly straighten out and extend your arms. If the rigging is not vertical and you're an inch off . . . you fall. Flyers work with a net and learn how to land high up on the shoulder blades but even so the impact is hard enough to cause damage."

After the Nelsons broke up, Bobby Kay went back to clowning, a step he has never regretted. "I started out as an acrobatic clown," he told me, "doing little hokum things like getting hit in the rear with a broom and doing a back flip or a full forward off the edge of a table."

I asked him how it felt to be a working clown, playing two shows a day for six months with a big circus.

"I always felt that the circus was my home," Bobby replied. "And when people come to my home it's up to me to be a good host. It's both my job and my pleasure to say, 'Welcome, I'm glad you came.' Oh, I may be tired after doing the same thing 'spontaneously' over and over again for six months but when the music starts everyone is on full point, ready to go. There's no use to cloud up on people, because you can't rain."

And on the subject of circus music:

"Clowns don't own watches. If you asked me the time right now I couldn't tell you because I've been brought up to think of the music as time. The circus band runs on a stopwatch and every performer can listen to it and tell exactly what act is on and how far along it is; we take our cues from hand signals but time our walk-around by listening to the music. If the show's pace is thrown off by an accident or a missed trick, the clowns will get an emergency 'wave-around' to go on and entertain extemporaneously—to become carpet clowns—while the gap is filled. You have to know something about clowning to do that."

Every year when the big show hits Los Angeles Bobby and his friend Harold Hall (neat whiteface) give a big party attended by upwards of two hundred circus people. It's a unique affair that probably brings together more veteran clowns in one place than any other event. I talked to one old-time clown who asked to remain

anonymous because he is still with the circus. He occasionally works as a "come-in clown" on the smaller mud shows that continue to roam the Middle West and South; but in the thirties and forties he did the same job for the big shows.

"Well, the big show has gone respectable now," he confided. "But in the old days we used to do pretty well working the 'connection'—that's the long corridor lined with concessions and sideshow tents between the place you first pay your admission and the big top itself.

"Come-in clowns greeted the people waiting in line to buy their entrance ticket. The folks thought it was great, these clowns coming right out for free to make the kids laugh. Well"—my companion, whom I'll call Rippo, smiled—"we were there to make the kids laugh all right but not for free. In those days—you may be old enough to remember—the ticket-wagon counter was always at the adult's eye level. Even if you were tall, you kind of had to get up on your toes to get your change.

"And there was always change. That was the idea. Tickets were priced $1.35 or $2.18 or some such crazy number so that if the customer handed up a ten-dollar bill he always got back some folding money and a whole pile of change. Now the circus is an exciting place—leastwise it used to be—and here's this honest-to-God clown *up close* making the kids run off in all directions with Mom and Dad all flustered trying to keep track of everybody; the change lying up there on the shelf is often missed or, if the buyer grabs it, it's probably not correct. The excess is scooped aside with a quick, practiced motion and at the end of the day the come-in clown, ticket taker, and circus owner could share as much as forty or fifty dollars, big money in those days.

"We used to call the 'connection' the 'shit shute,'" Rippo continued as he sipped liquid provided from our hosts' well-stocked bar, "because the lavatories were always located right at the end so that people who worked up a head of steam getting past the concessions and sideshows would have to stop at the johns; that would give the talkers a last chance at the others waiting their turn outside.

"The come-in clown would encourage the kids to take his hand

and walk with him over to the concessions while Dad was trying to figure out his change at the ticket wagon. Everything was priced crazy there, too. Like thirty-seven cents for this or sixty-four cents for that. The novelty salesmen were the worst. They would shout their wares, then drop their voices to a whisper at the price. People would get shortchanged right and left, buying stuff they didn't want because the clown had set the kids up."

Rippo shook his head ruefully. "It ain't like that any more," he said, "what with Ticketron and the big show wanting it to be a society evening with everyone wearing shirts and ties."

My friend had a point. The big circus feels that a higher class of people able to afford the rising ticket prices now attends the show and, treating it as a social outing, dresses accordingly. This new dignity may not be in keeping with the traditional function of the circus, the presentation of unsophisticated entertainment. People tend to shed their enjoyment inhibitions in inverse ratio to the formality of their dress.

"Why"—Rippo's face lit up—"I remember one mud show I worked not *that* long ago where the ticket guy set up a perfectly legit sign that said in small letters *Matinee* and in great big ones *3:00.* That was the time of the matinee. You'd be surprised at the number of folks who would come up and lay down three dollars expecting no change when the ticket price was really two-fifty." Rippo chuckled. "If the mark got sore and came back demanding his change, the ticket man would have a half-dollar all waiting for him, saying that he had walked away and left it there. Most often the mark would apologize."

Before the reader gets all choked up expressing moral indignation at these antics, let's permit ourselves the luxury of some idle speculation. What is a circus all about? It is a place of released inhibitions, unguarded laughter, and the willing suspension of disbelief. Perhaps *every* lion in that center ring isn't a vicious man-eater waiting for that one lapse in vigilance (occurring, hopefully, while we are there) on the trainer's part to tear him limb from limb.

Just possibly the flyer is not the world's foremost trapeze artist. Perhaps it isn't such a big deal as all that to the tiger who jumps through the burning hoop. Maybe the guy being shot out of the cannon isn't in *that* much danger. Who cares? If the ringmaster says it's so, it's so as far as we're concerned.

And the sideshow. Remember the sideshow? If you enjoyed the circus, that really *was* an Egyptian mummy you paid an extra quarter to see; and the cat lady didn't just need a shave; and Tom Thumb wasn't simply a millionaire midget; and the tallest man in the world was, simply, that.

But the new age of enlightenment is upon us and the sideshow is gone. The ringmaster now announces, for God's sake, an aerial ballet consisting of a bevy of Las Vegas-style, gorgeously costumed girls hanging on to some dangling ropes.

One thing is certain, we no longer have to worry about being bamboozled into enjoying ourselves or of having the good-natured satisfaction of being able to admit at home that someone had put one over on us during the performance or down the "shit shute." We are safe at the circus these days, antiseptically safe. Occasionally a smaller mud show will sneak a magic-potion salesman or a pea-shell game into the concession line, but we don't have to worry about matching wits with the pitchman; the law will compensate for our gullibility and curtail our enjoyment.

Remember the wonderful gag where two clowns come out each carrying a bucket. One starts chasing the other and just as they near the lower seats the pursuer heaves a bucketful of water all over his partner. The pursued becomes the pursuer, catches his prey right at the seats, draws his bucket back to get even, and, as the other clown ducks, heaves a bucketful of shavings into the first four or five screaming rows of the audience. No matter how many times you've seen that routine you duck and yell at the prospect of getting wet. Well, you probably will never watch that gag again and the reason why tells the whole story about the change in circus entertainment.

The big shows have issued explicit orders that the audience is not to be directly involved in any way with clown gags. One of those shavings might hit someone in the eye and a lawsuit could result. But it's worse than that, really. The circus believes that you and I no longer want to be bothered with corny gags. According to

Two stars: Pearl Bailey and Lou Jacobs behind the Big Top.

market-analysis studies we have become too sophisticated to be: *a)* fooled by anything so simplistic, and *b)* involved with anything that makes us personal participants. How anyone who watches a television game show can consider either premise valid is beyond me.

The big circus doesn't want its customers bothered by the entertainers. It aims for a "dressed-up" audience who regard the circus as a performance in much the same manner as legitimate theater or an ice-show extravaganza. The big show is dehumanizing itself by introducing basketball-playing unicycle riders and chorus girls in revealing costumes and by making sure that you and I get exact change.

Actress-singer-dancer Carol Lawrence visits backstage with Coco and Bobby Kay.

Academy Award nominee actress Diahann Carroll clowns it up with Coco and Bobby Kay during a benefit performance.

Forget the sideshow. That will never come back, because television, often unwittingly, has shown us real-life freaks that make the bearded lady seem as commonplace as a female Congressperson. But the big show itself is changing with the times and in so doing is quite possibly adapting itself out of existence.

There is one constant, however, in this evolutionary pattern: the clowns. And, according to many people with whom I have spoken in the preparation of this book, in their gloved hands lies the ultimate fate of the circus.

9
CLASSIC
ROUTINES

Wherever there are clowns there are gags. From small bits of light-in-the-nose business to elaborate mechanical contrivances like the exploding car that drives itself, the basic clown routines have not changed over the years. Although new ideas are constantly introduced (Harry Ross uses a "television camera" in one of his walk-arounds, for example), the classic gags seen by succeeding generations are what carry on the clown tradition.

This repetition is deliberate. Anyone who has gone to a circus over a sixty-year span can share his or her experience with anyone else, no matter if each saw different shows twenty-five years apart. A fifty-year-old can relive his reaction to the exploding-car gag in the company of a ten-year-old seeing it for the first time, and each will get the same kick out of the clowns' antics. And that, many people believe, is one of the big reasons for the circus's longevity.

"The reason we repeat those routines with almost no change," George "Perky" Perkins explains, "is that we realize that one of the thrills of seeing the circus over and over again with children and grandchildren is to watch the kids' reactions; seeing the youngsters get the same enjoyment out of the house-on-fire as we did thirty years ago adds to our enjoyment of seeing it again ourselves."

A psychologist might say that watching clowns represents one of the few chances offered different generations for a shared experience, and that is probably true. But it is in the doing that the shared experience takes on the special dimension that the clown is talking about. If you've ever taken a younger person to a circus think a moment about your own reactions.

Here they come! The painter carrying the long board walks up behind his buddy bending over a bucket, intent on mixing paint. Momentarily distracted the board-carrier turns, swinging his board in a wide arc until it swats the stirrer with a resounding whack and dumps him headfirst into the bucket. Everyone watching is delighted, the repeat viewer because he knows a lot more is going to happen with that board, the young first-timer because it's all new to him.

The inept painters and their board, actually two thin boards fastened at one end to form a slapstick (the origin of the term), make

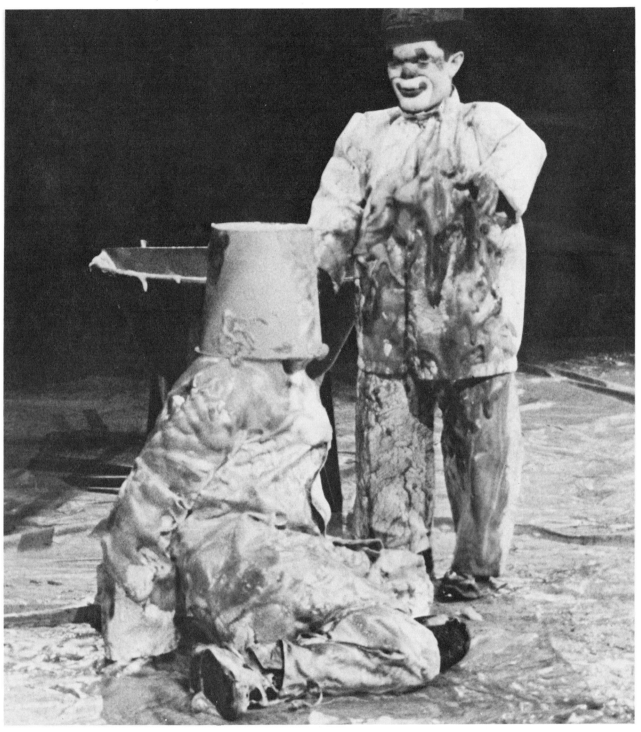

Of all the traditional clown routines the inept painters perhaps strike closest to home. Here midget clown Frankie Saluto surveys his handiwork. Dumping the bucket with apparent spontaneity while avoiding injuring his partner requires painstaking rehearsal and split-second timing.

South African clown Billy Levinsohn shows that it plays the same in Peoria and Pretoria.

A great clown prop. In the midst of chaos a "painter's" hat suddenly squirts "paint" high in the air. A pressure bulb concealed in the clown's purposefully oversize costume forces the colored water to impressive heights.

us laugh both because of the routine itself and our anticipation of it. Clowns mean fun; we know that something amusing is going to happen and, if we also know what that something is, the knowledge heightens our pleasure.

Of course, sometimes we only think we know what is going on; very often things are happening right in front of our eyes that we do not see. Let's take a look at a couple of examples.

The whole point of the house-on-fire gag is rescuing the "mother and baby" from the second story of their burning home. We see the house catch fire and watch the agonizing calls for help from the upstairs window as "mother and child" keep falling back into the holocaust and reappearing for a few frenzied seconds. Actually the "mother" is jumping up-and-down on a trampoline concealed inside, but that is a technical matter. It is the unscheduled events—as much a surprise to the clowns as to the audience—that we often fail to perceive.

The famous fire truck complete with "mother" whiteface Dick Lewis and always-rescued "baby" on the Russell Brothers show, circa 1940.

The fire truck comes rushing to the rescue, a fireman with an axe seemingly imbedded in his head hooks up a hose whose nozzle squirts backward, and the gag is on. Organized pandemonium reigns as "mother" becomes more hysterical and various firemen rush up with ladders, axes, or whatever else is at hand to get the job done.

Now, at one particular performance, let's stop the action as the clown grabs the hose and rushes to connect it to a hydrant. Out of the corner of his eye he spots the chimp act being wheeled up in a tarpaulin-covered wagon. Normally the chimps, to perform next in that ring, would be held back until the house-on-fire gag had been cleared from the arena. And with good cause. For some reason that has never been adequately explained chimps hate all clowns.

"Maybe it's the unreal face," one clown theorized, "or the costume or a combination of both, but when the chimp act is coming back from the ring you'll see any clowns that are standing around duck behind a pole or jump up on top of a trunk or something. Those chimps, especially the bigger ones, can be real mean."

On this occasion the chimp trainer misses his cue and is out in the performing area while the clowns are furiously running around the blazing house. The axe-head clown does his elaborate pantomime of attaching the hose to the hydrant with one eye on the chimps. The tarpaulin covers the wagon, shielding the chimps from the audience's view but, chimps being chimps, they raise up the lower edge and peek.

The hydrant is next to their wagon and the combination of noise, motion, and a clown jumping around with a hose right near them is too much for the simians. In an instant the tarp is off and the entire chimp act jumps out and heads for the fireman. His reaction is immediate; he drops the hose and runs for a rope ladder hanging down from the trapeze rigging, with six chimps on his tail. The crowd is roaring with laughter at this surprise twist. The fireman just gets his hands on the bottom rung when the chimps hit him, dragging him down. They roll over and over in the sawdust, the clown kicking and flailing his arms and the chimps trying to bite him with their strong teeth. Fortunately his clothing is loose and he is agile. He gains his feet and takes refuge behind the chimp trainer, who is ordering his charges back to the wagon.

While all this is going on, the other clowns, despite their anxiety, are completing the house-on-fire gag and the crowd is gasping for breath—that last bit with the clown hiding behind the trainer was too much: great circus fun and a laugh they will remember for a long time.

When the clown gets back to the dressing area, he has teeth marks on both legs and his costume is ripped to shreds. The chimp trainer checks him over and is relieved to find no broken skin. The trainer then turns on a big chimp who led the attack, picks up a length of lead pipe, and admonishes him for his lack of discipline by hitting him on the head with a blow that would fell any man. The chimp merely blinks, shakes his head, and frowns his puzzlement at this unseemly treatment.

But something else has been happening during all this commotion that increased the crowd's pleasure and brought on much laughter. The clown "mother" who is jumping up and down on the trampoline inside the house strains to see if his colleague has escaped the chimps. (All this, remember, without the audience being aware of anything wrong.) His concern throws his timing off so he whips the cover off the lycopodium pot prematurely. Instead of erupting into more smoke and flame, the gas, having insufficient build-up time to create enough volume to explode, escapes as gas and the clown gets two lungfuls that send him into a paroxym of coughing and gagging even as he continues his leaping routine.

The audience sees this and reacts with wholehearted approval; obviously the "mother" is nearly overcome, making her immediate rescue all the more pressing. Fortunately the lycopodium gas causes only discomfort—its inhalation is not an uncommon occurrence —and hours later the clown is none the worse for wear.

If you had been in the audience that night, would you have really known what you were looking at? And that kind of thing happens all the time.

Clowns, probably because of their own awareness, are great chimp-storytellers. "I remember back with the Cole Brothers Circus," one clown reminisced before a show. "We had this music conductor, a great big guy who stuck out in that red-and-gold uniform as he stood up there leading the band. One of the chimps, Sara I think her name was, took a dislike to him. Night after night she'd sit there waiting to go on, watching him. Clowns notice things like that," he explained with a grin. "Especially where chimps are concerned.

By the time this squad got through, the drill sergeant had to be carried off on a stretcher. Sensitive to anything that suggests controversy the circus now shies away from military routines.

"Well, the show had run for nearly three months and every night was the same. Sara would sit there gazing at this guy waving his arms around; if you didn't know chimps you'd think she was in love with him. Then one night the act—I think they were Mickey Antalek's chimps, but I'm not sure—was running out and Sara took off. Before anyone was even aware of it—they can be very fast, you know—Sara had this guy by the ankles, one in each hand. She flipped him up in the air over her head; he did at least one somersault and landed flat on his back near the first ring." The clown chuckled. "He had all the wind knocked out of him but was back for the second show. I guess Sara caught hell for that."

Dog acts, too, are very wary of chimps. A chimp will reach out faster than your eye can follow, grab a dog, and flip him fifty or a hundred feet into the air just for laughs. Usually the animal doesn't survive; dog trainers take a dim view of that kind of humor.

Although unplanned and sometimes near-fatal action converted by the clowns' professionalism into a gag is an exciting concept, the day-to-day mechanics of some of the well-known routines, although less spectacular, are not without interest.

Take Perky's famous exploding, self-driving car, for example. George Perkins, like Bobby Kay, has been in the circus nearly all his professional life. Living today in semi-retirement in the beautiful Southern California mountain village of Yucaipa, Perky started out by selling tickets in Venice, California, in 1918. He was soon making props and gags for other clowns and was in fact "producing" before he became a clown. Perky built and worked his first car for the L.G. Barnes Show in 1929. With a few memory jogs from his charming wife Gai, Perky recalled that first routine.

"The car comes out with me at the wheel," he began, "but I'm not really driving, although the audience doesn't know that. It goes a little way and the engine starts coughing. A cop stops me and I get out and go round front to check and see what's the matter.

"Water squirts up out of the radiator and I get an umbrella, but when I open it the thing explodes and I run around to the rear of the car in panic. It starts to backfire and some Roman candles we have hidden there go off, hitting me in the stomach. I'm wearing

Perky (right) with his son Terry, the unseen driver who was a key part of the act.

The famous exploding car, one of four designed and built by tramp George "Perky" Perkins over a forty-year span. "Cop" Renee Thezan was the tramp's longtime partner. The third team member who drove the "driverless" car was never seen by the audience.

a big fur coat with a special protective lining. There are ten balls of fire in all, and each time one hits me I do a pratfall." Perky's pleasant face broke into a smile. "That's a very rigorous part of the act," he recalled.

"Well, I get back in the car and very carefully wipe the windshield. The cop points to a spot I missed and I stick my head all the way through to get a better look. No glass. I reach down and get a bottle out of a mailbox stuck on the outside of the door. The cop taps me on the shoulder and I spit my drink into a cuspidor on the running board, making smoke and flames shoot out. I'll tell you how all these things are controlled in a minute.

"I get back in the car and am all ready to go when a tire blows. I get out and start pumping up the tire. All of a sudden the car, trailing explosions and smoke, takes off on its own and chases the cop all the way around the track only to come back and stop exactly where it was before. I go back to pumping the tire as though nothing has happened; a big explosion knocks me flat underneath the car.

"The cop bends over, looking for me. I appear back up in the seat and swat him on the rear with a broom; he falls and I do a full forward somersault onto the track. The car takes off with me hanging on to the spare tire and the cop hanging on to my pants which he pulls off just as we all exit." Perky smiled his satisfaction at reliving the gag that has changed very little over the years. "I built four of those cars," he told me, "and improved each one a little bit."

His son, Terry, now a strapping six foot two, actually drove the car from a precarious perch over the rear axle, his visibility limited to a concealed slit in the rear seat's back upholstery. Terry had two jobs: he drove the car with a steering wheel, forward and reverse gear (lack of space prevented the installation of a brake; he used reverse for that function), and he triggered the gags as his father went through the act.

"In the very old days," Perky recalls, "there was a set of fuses up in front of the driver that he touched off with a match or lighter but I rigged up a little switchboard that worked off the car battery; all Terry had to do was flip each switch at the right time. The umbrella was the only one that didn't work off a switch; I touched that off myself with a cigar."

Young Perkins actually learned to drive in Perky's car, and as he grew adjustments had constantly to be made in foot-pedal and steering-wheel length until his legs stretched way out under the car. The first time he ever saw the act was when he left the show to go into the Army. "Say, Dad," he told his father, "that really is a very funny routine!"

Perky was the producing clown on the William Tell gag, variations of which have been part of nearly every circus that has played over the past thirty years.

Perky, carrying a rifle, and another clown stop during their walk-around. Perky makes an elaborate pantomime of setting a glass of water on his buddy's head. Every time Perky turns his back to ready his gun the other guy takes a quick drink of water. By the time Perky has the gun in working order the glass in nearly empty. He demands to know where the water went and the other clown points to his stomach. Perky takes careful aim, fires, and water squirts out front and back of the target's middle where the bullet has supposedly passed through.

The secret: A special water-filled rubber tube designed and made by Perky that fits around the straight-man's waist; front and rear valves arc activated when he squeezes a concealed bulb.

Perhaps few gags typify the continuity of the circus better than the tiny car that circles the track and inexplicably disgorges a great many clowns, animals, and inanimate objects. When I was a youngster I used to think the car stopped over a trapdoor in the floor but, after going back to see the same show two or three times, I decided that there couldn't be that many trapdoors scattered throughout the big top. I was a very bright child.

Bobby Kay, who was producing clown on that routine for many years, talks about it.

"Well, that gag was pure clown and pure circus," he told me. "The best we ever had on that were twenty-two clowns, a pony, and a bass drum that I squeezed into a car about the size of a small Honda."

I asked him how it was done.

"Well, it's not really a trick in the sense of being an illusion. It's really a matter of organization. Everyone is stacked spoon-fash-

Organ-grinder Del LeClair and cop Al Darrow rehearse a walk-around routine. The gent with the tin cup is "Perky" Perkins in an unusual nonclown appearance.

ion. I must say"—Kay chuckled—"it can get pretty ripe in there. The car is stripped inside and the driver sits directly on the frame with his legs dangling down, sometimes scraping the ground.

"The clown costumes are especially designed to expand when the wearer stands up so he looks just that much bigger than he is. For instance, one clown might have a metal umbrella-frame sewn into his coat; when he raises his arms the whole coat blows up like a balloon."

The car act has to be choreographed, with every move and position planned and rehearsed in advance. Behind the entrance curtain everything is arranged so that twenty-two clowns, pony, and bass drum begin stacking up with just enough time to slam the doors and respond to the music cue.

"As you get older, smarter, and have more seniority," Bobby added, "you get to be the last one in and, of course, the first one out."

How many more inside? A mini-version of the small-car routine. Note the oversize clothes to further the illusion of big out of small.

BRING ON THE CLOWNS

When Ernest Borgnine, appearing as a clown in a Fourth-of-July parade, rode atop a wagon with Lou Jacobs, he was astonished at the crowd's failure to recognize the famous clown. "I couldn't believe it," the motion-picture star told me. "Here I was feeling privileged to ride and work with Lou and the spectators didn't even know who he was!"

That one incident sums up the fate of the performing American clown. It may be deemed unhappy in the sense that he is denied public recognition and the personal fame and, of course, money that follow. Viewed philosophically the modern clown's anonymity may be a blessing in whiteface, sparing him the emotional strains that often accompany public acclaim.

It may be argued that the clown can blame his lack of identity on the very medium whose success he did so much to further, the circus. When circuses were small, one-ring affairs with a minimal seating capacity the clown was heard as well as seen. As late as the 1870s he spoke to the audience, often incorporating newsworthy topics, and sang lyrics that frequently satirized contemporary politics.

The singing clown was an important fixture of the small circus. Each had its featured clown and published a songster, a small, pocket-sized booklet containing both currently popular songs and the specialties of the show's singing star. Often the clown himself sold these songsters before the performance, pocketing a portion of the proceeds, which was sometimes his only pay for the day's work.

The Forepaugh-Sells Circus featured clowns like Sam Long singing "Castles in the Air" and put out elaborate songsters with color covers that sold for twenty-five cents, more than the circus program itself. The How's Great London Circus published a songster in the 1860s that featured the great Irish singing clown Johnny Patterson, whose rendition of "I Met Her in the Garden where the Praties Grow" (praties, by the way, are potatoes) is said to have been a classic of its kind.

W.W. Cole, of Cole's Circus, Museum and Trained Animal Exposition operating in the 1890s, had outgrown the singing clown; nonetheless, he saw fit to publish a songster in 1894, perhaps be-

In the tradition of the great nineteenth-century singing clowns: Karl Waddell, classic in whiteface and costume.

JOHN LOWLOW,
Great Talking Clown,

WITH

JOHN ROBINSON'S

10 Big Shows all Combined.

SONGSTER

N.Y. POPULAR PUB. CO. 37 BOND St. NEW YORK.

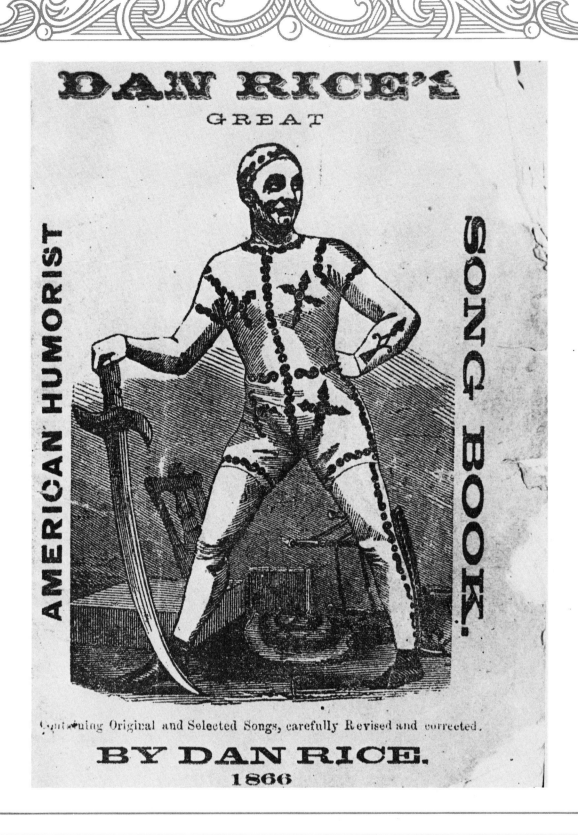

The front covers of two "songsters" from the era when clowns sang, told jokes, and made political commentary.

cause the public expected one even though there were no singing clowns with the circus. Gradually the songster became incorporated into the circus program, but the nostalgia it evoked caused the Hagenbeck-Wallace Circus to publish one in 1918 that contained the words and lyrics of popular songs of the day; by that time the big top had outgrown the vocal range of the singing clown.

Other great singing clowns and their specialties include Charlie Parker singing "Lannigan's Ball" with the Yankee Robinson Circus, Billy Andrews doing "I Will Never Kiss My Girl Again Behind the Kitchen Door" for John Robinson's Excelsior Circus, and Jerry Hopper rendering "Old Dog Tray" with P.A. Older's Circus in the 1870s.

We have already discussed how monologists such as Dan Rice, Will Rogers, and Bob Hope became logical extensions of the vocal clown. Rogers, incidentally, worked with the Werth Circus in Australia early in his career. Stranded when a touring vaudeville troupe went broke, Rogers joined Werth, Australia's largest circus, and toured South Africa with it, doing his rope tricks. Soon after that he returned to the United States and went on stage as a "single," padding his act with the patter that was to become his trademark and make him famous.

Television has provided yet another logical extension of the talking clown in the glib, knowledgeable talk-show host exemplified by Johnny Carson and Merv Griffin. Carson, with an opening, topical monologue, followed by often barbed comments throughout the program as he chats with guests about the contemporary scene, has in fact shaped a whole new commentator-comic art form that, in effect, puts him in the single ring of the small mid-nineteenth-century circus playing to a tent magically packed with millions of people.

Around the 1870s the circus's growing popularity (based in no small part on its clowns) and the general trend toward bigness that we have discussed elsewhere opened up the big top so that an individual clown's voice was unable to reach a large part of the audience. He adapted to his expanded surroundings by broadening his sight gags—by learning to work "high"—and by developing rou-

tines that would be easy to follow no matter where one sat. An anonymous 1922 author writing in a circus program describes what happened:

"The one, the only, the inimitable clown that used to be a character of such importance that his name was heralded in lithographic splendor, is gone, but a horde of just as clever and more vigilant cut-ups has replaced him.

"The funny old clown who sang the comic song, reeled off quip and conundrum and made the ringmaster ridiculous, has become a medley, a multitude of abstracts, a whirlwind of unidentified comedy, catering to all ages.

"The reason is quite obvious. The arena is so large that no one clown can be the cynosure of all eyes, the privileged jester whose sole efforts stand out conspicuously and individually. There must needs be a small army of the chalk-faced laugh-producers in order to simultaneously amuse the great audiences."

The clown emphasis shifted from the clown to the gag. Rabid circus fans continue to match a famous clown face with a name, but the identifiable clown is fast becoming extinct. Clown schools, whether located in Florida or San Diego, with rare exceptions are merely supplying people who look like clowns and who are technically capable of performing clown routines. Today the gag is the thing. Perhaps what is needed is an about-face in circus policy that would permit the emergence of a new generation of clown stars. True, they would probably command more money than is at present earned, but would they not, like stars in other branches of show business, draw an audience that would justify their salaries?

For now, however, we have a legacy of gags that will guarantee continued enjoyment of clown comedy even though the individual clowns may not be as accomplished as some of their predecessors.

Although an established clown face generally is spared duplication, clown gags are not. Every circus above the mud-show level has a clown fire brigade, and countless versions of Perky's exploding car have steered themselves around the arena. Trying to trace the true origin of a clown routine is something akin to pinning down the name of the first circus to use electricity. A number of people seem to have gotten the same idea around the same time. (As far as electricity goes, the Cooper-Bailey Circus featured a demonstration of *ELECTRIC LIGHT* as one of their sideshow attractions in 1880, charging an extra fee is you wanted to view the generator. It would appear, however, that circus illumination gradually evolved from gas to electricity with no single, abrupt transition recorded.)

Some single gags remain indelibly impressed on the memory as being associated with a specific clown. Felix Adler with his enormous behind and tiny umbrella; Buzzy Potts and his two amazing little dogs who would follow him during his walk-around, disappearing only suddenly to reappear riding on a tiny ledge attached to his backside; Dick Ford, perhaps the archetypical clown cop; Emmett Kelly and his big mallet that always crushed the little peanut; Lou Jacobs taking a bath in his self-propelled tub; Gene Lewis as a lady clown; Jackie Gerlich a "baby" being wheeled through the walk-around with a cigar stuck in his mouth; Griebling and Fred Freeman with their flat leather "boxing gloves" that made such satisfying noise when making contact.

Every clown fan undoubtedly has his favorite recollection of the walk-around. Production numbers are harder to pin down, because they usually involved more than one clown and were often borrowed freely by competing circuses. It is fairly certain, however, that Bobby Kay more than twenty years ago was the producing clown who first presented the reducing gag that has since become a part of circus lore.

The gag begins with a small, emaciated-looking clown coming out and heading purposefully for a large square box clearly marked "Reducing Cabinet." "You learn," Bobby explained, "how to sort of cave in and walk small so that you lose several inches off your normal height."

With the audience's approval he enters the cabinet but, instead of reducing, he begins to put on weight. He makes several trips outside to puzzle over his predicament but, at the crowd's urging, he keeps going back in until, finally, he gets so fat that he bursts out

Gene Lewis, one of the great clown female impressionists.

The boxing gag. The flat bladders are slapped together with deceptive swiftness by the "victim" to create a resounding whacking sound as the aggressor supposedly smacks his face: (left to right) Otto Griebling, Jackie Gerlich, Fred Freeman.

the sides of the cabinet and runs, confused and embarrassed, for the exit.

Bobby had a special suit made, consisting of a long-underwear type of garment lined on the outside with plastic and an ordinary-appearing outer suit lined on the inside with plastic. The two plastic linings were carefully sealed at all openings and the sealed section had an air valve concealed on the inside of one elbow. Once in the cabinet the clown would hook up with an air compressor concealed under the flooring. It was virtually impossible to make the suit completely airtight and Bobby had to time his exit so that any escaping air wouldn't put him on a quick reducing diet before he left the arena.

Clown gags, although usually very broad in order to be seen by everyone, occasionally rely on illusion to gain their effect. These stage-magician type of routines have to be played bigger than life to be effective in the circus, so their application is limited. One of the best is the doll-house gag, in which an impossibly tiny house suddenly sprouts a full-grown clown. Unlike the tiny-car gag that depends upon planning and physical agility, the doll house deceives the eye through its trick staging.

The house is usually set way up off the floor on a table that has at least thirty-six-inch legs, thus heightening the illusion of smallness and making trickery seem less likely. The opposite, of course, is the case. The table "top," painted and designed to blend in with the legs, is really the bottom of the house. The house is painted in gaudy stripes that appear uniform but actually are broader in the front than back, giving an illusion of shallowness where there is actually depth and height.

When the house is brought out, the concealed clown is riding in it with his legs and behind in the table top and his torso and head up in the false rear wall that, because of the stripe-created optical effect, appears to have no thickness. At a signal a puff of smoke erupts, the roof swings back on a hinge, and an incredibly large clown stands up in a space that seems fit to hold only his ankles and feet. He has pushed the false rear wall forward to form a new, higher floor while wriggling upright on his toes to give himself added height. Meantime the audience doesn't realize that the clowns who have carried the table out and are now expressing their amazement are all holding their bodies low to add to the central illusion. That ability to drop the body and "take a set" is the result of long training and discipline; an experienced clown can shorten himself by a couple of inches without appearing to make any kind of movement.

Almost without exception every veteran clown I have met—whether still working full-time in his early sixties or semi-retired in his early seventies—seemed to me to be in better physical condition than someone of comparable age engaged in a more sedentary occupation. The walk-around itself is demanding enough, but most of the gags involve a lot of jumping about that can quickly sap a clown's energies. Most of us look at a clown as being ageless, and rightly so; but being ageless means not showing weariness or any of the other signs of human involvement. One story illustrates our often unconscious feelings about clowns and how they, in turn, are subject to pressures like everyone else.

I was standing just behind the entrance curtain of a small circus still playing under canvas. A clown, an auguste old-timer who was nearing the end of a two-show-a-day three-month run, was waiting to go on. He was working the balloon-exploding act alone, which meant that he had not only to blow up a balloon five times during the walk-around and make it explode, but he had to do all the pantomiming to the audience so they would urge him on to greater efforts. I knew he was tired and that he was "getting it all together" to perform the demanding routine with the enthusiasm expected of him.

A small boy, the son of some local official permitted backstage, was pestering the clown with questions. Then the kid started pulling at the tail of the clown's oversized cutaway coat; I could tell that the performer's patience was wearing thin. Straining to hear his music cue he pulled away somewhat abruptly from the youngster who, undaunted, came up with a final question. "Do clowns," he asked, "have to take a bath like a hooman bein'?" It broke the clown up. He laughed, reached down and patted his little fan on the head, heard his cue, and ran, seemingly bubbling with energy, onto the track.

That about sums it up for most of us: clowns are simply not "hooman bein's."

When an acrobat, for example, adds a clown costume and face to a routine he gets an extra, crowd-pleasing dimension. He is no longer simply performing a physical feat, no matter how intricate or daring; his audience finds a humorous satisfaction in the knowledge that a *clown* can outperform mere mortals. A stilt walker excites our admiration as he makes his ungainly way around the arena; add a clown face to the precipitous perambulator and the act becomes both interesting and amusing. The famous rocking tables, done for so many years by Harry Rittley, features a clown-acrobat on a kitchen chair high atop a column of tables. He rocks backward and forward until the whole tower is so far off the vertical as to seemingly defy gravity until he finally falls forward, adding a big triple somersault—another routine that somehow takes on added meaning when done by a clown.

Clowns who are not "hooman bein's" cannot very well be lady or man clowns, either. However, since up to the present writing there are two distinct sexes, wherever there are clowns there are females who, for one reason or another, wish to be clowns. Should a female who becomes a clown make herself into a neutral—that is, male—clown or should she preserve her identity so that she is readily identifiable in face and costume?

In the old days that was never any problem. Women joined the circus as clowns to be with their clown husbands or as part of a family act. Circus life was tough enough without having unattached girls vying for space in the men's dressing tent; would-be female clowns didn't fare too well on the ladies' side of Broadway, because there was no clown alley to keep their powder from billowing over the often elaborate costumes of other female performers.

Though husband-and-wife clown acts have always been a part of the circus, the audience was usually unaware of the fact. Grace and Jack Fairburn worked the walk-around with Grace costumed as a kind of whiteface auguste wearing top hat and tails, and the fans were none the wiser. Felix and Amelia Adler, Dime and Connie Wilson (whose son Little Dime became a part of their act), were similar clown teams.

A clown leads the always spectacular stilt-walkers around the arena.

Can you pick out the early '40s husband-wife clown team? The high silk hat and the neat whiteface crouching at lower right are Grace and Jack Fairburn, a pioneering combination. At extreme left is Art Larue, one of the better-known clown cops. George Perkins, still developing costume and face, stands between Larue and Mrs. Fairburn.

During the days of the canvas big top a number of male clowns got themselves up as females; a clown being a girl was always good for a big laugh. Dick Lewis is a contemporary example of a vanishing breed.

The fact that clowns who looked like girls got laughs for that reason alone does not sit too well with today's women-libbers. Actually the clown female impersonators are a great tribute to the art of clowning itself. Performers like Dick Lewis could and can do that sort of thing (Lou Jacobs does a great "mother," pushing a carriage containing a midget clown) without the opprobrium attached to "drag" entertainers in specialized night clubs. The greasepaint artists are above suspicion because, quite simply, their motives are pure.

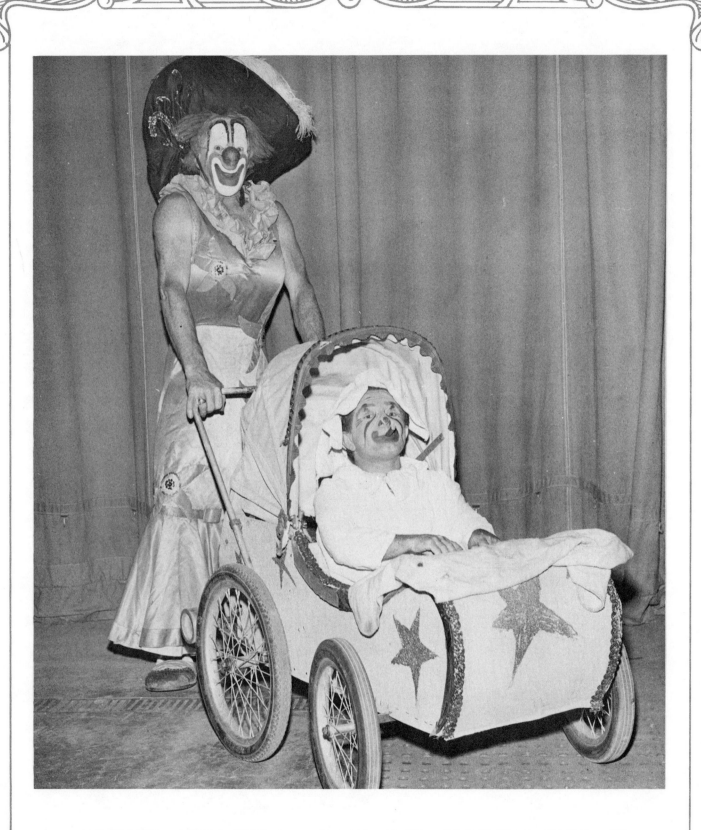

Lou Jacobs waits to wheel cigar-chomping Jackie Gerlich through the walk-around. Great clowns like Jacobs and Gene Lewis can make comedy of female impersonation, rather than a "drag"-oriented act—a fast-dying art.

Of late, with the advent of clown schools and the doctrine of sexual parity, women clowns are distinctly recognizable as females. Peggy Williams and Barbara Nadell are hard-working clowns who ask no quarter in the two-a-day grind of the long circus season. One has to ask, however, whether or not their obvious sexual identification interferes with the traditional role of the clown.

"I think it's fine for a girl clown to get the idea across in her hair and face especially," Harold Hall, a neat whiteface forty-year-plus circus veteran told me. "I feel she shouldn't have any special privileges, shouldn't work less or not do certain things, just because she's a woman. But I don't see anything wrong in letting people know she's a she."

Yet this writer, who doesn't quite have Harold's seniority and is far from a traditionalist in other things, can't help but think, whenever he sees Peggy or Barbara or any of their contemporaries working: "Hey, there's a girl clown." And that thought, I submit, destroys the illusion.

There are gags where lady clowns, taking the place of male clowns dressed like women, fit right in, provided they are playing a specific character role, i.e., lady clown, for that one routine.

In the washing machine gag a whole gaggle of clowns all carrying their laundry in hampers descend on a single washing machine. They begin arguing over who will do the washing first and the scene is soon erupting with thrown clothes, hampers, and soap flakes as everyone goes berserk. Finally, as a compromise, all the others turn on a midget clown—perhaps Prince Paul Horompo, Mike Padilla or Frankie Saluto—pick him up and throw him into the machine. Lady clowns are quite welcome here, although the rough-and-tumble acrobatics can be strenuous. Incidentally, although a large proportion of "midget" clowns are actually dwarfs, the latter term is never used; any adult, abnormally small clown is always called a midget by show people.

The most famous circus midget of all time was not a clown. Tom Thumb, discovered and exploited by P. T. Barnum, in addition to being the most publicized midget ever to appear with a circus, was probably the most accomplished. Perfectly formed, standing a

Frankie Saluto learned a long time ago that makeup mirrors were placed for people, not midget clowns.

Movie star Wallace Beery lends a hand to Tom Thumb, the world's most famous, and wealthiest, midget.

full twenty-nine inches high, Thumb could sing and dance and had a captivating, outgoing personality. Though he was first exhibited more as a freak than a performer, it soon became obvious to his mentor that he could become a star in his own right. The often misused ballyhoo, "He entertained the crowned heads of Europe," really applied in Thumb's case. During three visits to England he was received at the Court of St. James's as a personal favorite of the king. In addition he was an invited guest to some of the most prestigious seats of European nobility and made millions of dollars for himself and Barnum.

Another routine, school days, lends itself to mixed clown company. A dozen or so clowns are seated at desks as the "teacher" begins the lesson at a blackboard. A couple of "pupils"—usually midget clowns—begin acting up and the others join in; soon the classroom is a shambles. The teacher vainly tries to restore order until, thoroughly cowed, he is chased out of the ring by the midget clowns, losing his pants in the process. Girl-clown pupils add a note of authenticity, although if they act too feminine they may spoil the slapstick nature of the act.

One aspect of clowning that the ladies would be hard put to master, if they wished to do so, would be that of the rodeo clown who combines the physical agility of the acrobat with the humor of his circus counterpart and adds a generous dash of danger. Those who would see tragedy and laughter behind the greasepaint façade will especially appreciate the dual roles of the rodeo clown. He is in the ring to preserve an appearance of lighthearted high jinks while performing a deadly serious, dangerous role. It is his job to distract an enraged bull from a thrown and frequently injured rodeo rider until the cowboy can be dragged to safety.

A new category must be created for the rodeo clown: hazardous tramp. He dresses with big, exaggerated tramp clothes that flap as he runs waving a big red bandana to attract the bull. The costume, designed to divert the animal's attention away from the downed rider, hampers the clown's movement and can slow him that half-step that is the difference between safety and serious injury. Rodeo clowns on the average are better paid than their circus cousins—

rodeo stars tip generously for their services—but their career span is short. When they feel their legs beginning to go they usually quit rather than risk matching the speed and agility of an enraged bull. Oddly enough, they normally do not go into some less-frenzied form of clowning; some have tried it but found it too difficult to adjust to the subtleties of more conventional clown humor.

A CLOWN
IS
SPECIAL

The clown enters the now deserted fifth-floor playroom of Children's Hospital in Los Angeles and Bobby Kay the man, whom we have come to know well through ten chapters, is lost to us. He carries a bagful of tricks—metal rings that magically separate, kerchiefs that tie and untie mysteriously, an elusive rabbit that keeps changing form behind a tiny wooden door, a bird in a cage that disappears, cage and all, before our very eyes—and his large splayed feet carry him from room to room as small faces, somber a moment before, light up with smiles. The circus has not passed them by, and they react eagerly to the clown's happy smile and constant chatter.

He approaches a boy whose bed is a mass of pulleys, counterweights, and tubes. His bike had been struck by a car, throwing him thirty feet through the air. On the critical list for the first three days he is still in constant pain because his system will not accept any more drugs. He lies on his side, unmoving, as the clown squats down and peers through the bars of the raised bedside. His grandmother, who has taken turns with his mother and father on a twenty-four-hour watch, looks on anxiously from the crowded doorway.

An interesting thing has happened since the clown began his rounds; nurses, aides, even doctors, have begun following this white-face Pied Piper from room to room, responding as the children do to his inexhaustible store of good cheer. They know the full measure of his magic because they are aware of the extent of their small charges' pain. Watching the adult professionals react is a revelation; this funny, happy, silly clown is transforming sickrooms into little pockets of joy and hope—a rare demonstration of wonderful, though fleeting, miracles.

"Do you feel like saying 'Hello'?" the clown asks.

After a moment the boy lowers his fingers from his eyes. He is crying, has been for four days and nights. Sometimes he screams aloud at the car to stop, just as he did at the moment of impact. Now he looks uncertainly through tear-filled eyes at the clown.

"Your grandma tells me you've been a brave boy."

The boy looks but gives no sign.

"I've brought a bunny rabbit to see you."

A hospital is suddenly a happy place for young Peter Trento.

The patient stares at the little wooden door pressed against the bars as the clown pretends to peek behind it.

"Yep, he's there all right. Want to see him?"

A hestitation, then a nod, yes.

The clown whips open the door and a picture of Mr. Rabbit stands revealed.

"See? He came all the way from the circus to see you."

The audience stares, interested.

"Now, watch." The door is closed and reopened and there stands *Mrs.* Rabbit.

The tears have stopped and the hand moves away from his face.

The clown closes the door.

"Would you like to see who's behind the door now?" He presses it closer to the bars. "There's the knob. You can open it and find out for yourself."

Slowly, tentatively, the hand slides across the pillow and touches the tiny doorknob.

"Go ahead," the clown urges.

The boy cautiously opens the door; both Mr. and Mrs. Rabbit have disappeared, leaving only a big bunny tail. A smile creeps slowly over the youngster's face, then, as the clown reacts with wide-eyed astonishment, the little boy laughs. Sharp intakes of breath and smiles from the adults please the clown more than any big-top applause. Somehow a corner has been turned; somehow even the professionally skeptical doctors and nurses know that pain will be eased and recovery speeded.

The grandmother kneels by the bed as the boy whispers into her ear. She turns and calls to the departing clown.

"Mr. Clown," she says, fighting back her joyful tears, "he wants to kiss you."

As the clown leans over and a small hand reaches up and shyly touches his face, more than one nurse turns away, dabbing at her eyes with tissue to remove some mysterious, invisible objects.

And that, really, is what this book is all about. We have tried to learn what makes an otherwise quite ordinary "hooman bein' "

into something so far removed from the human condition that we willingly let down our guards and, often despite ourselves, respond uninhibitedly in his presence. His simplicity is one key to his special status. He simplifies the complicated. In a society that seeks elaborately contrived explanations for very basic emotional problems the clown is a throwback, a refreshing anachronism. One walk-around by a covey of sawdust comedians probably releases as much tension as weeks of therapy at the hands of a clinical psychologist, para or otherwise.

One clown whacks another across the behind with a slapstick, sending him tumbling head over heels. That's funny. No ifs, ands, or buts. We don't have to be afraid to laugh. We're safe. No one is going to second-guess us and make us feel foolish. We're comfortable losing some of our protective emotional veneer and with it, albeit unwittingly, some of our painstakingly fabricated hang-ups.

Unfortunately, as the circus goes, so goes the clown. Not just any circus but the big circus that provided the continuity, resources, and audiences so necessary for the laborious honing process that has produced great American clowns like Paul Jung, Felix Adler, Paul Jerome, and the many others we have written about and portrayed in these pages. Not just any big circus but a circus steeped in tradition is needed; and, sadly, there does not seem to be one around. Shirley Carroll, a circus veteran who loves both the show and the clowns, observes that the emphasis on turning out assembly-line young clowns and getting rid of what an owner of a big circus has characterized as "old has-beens" is going to be fatal to both clown and circus.

There are, however, a surprising number of small shows around. Last season the San Francisco area was visited by no less than sixteen circuses. The Happytime Circus, Polack Brothers Circus, George Mathews Circus, John Strong's 1869 Circus, Circus Vargas, Rudy Brothers Circus, Emmett Kelly, Jr. Circus, Gatti-Charles Circus, Early American Circus, Europorama, Kay Brothers Circus, Ringling-Barnum's Blue Unit, Michael's Spaghetti Circus, Royal Lichtenstein Circus, De Wayne Brothers Circus, and PAL Circus all played the West Coast and most used clowns. During one perform-

An appreciative volunteer holds his cigar while Bob "Frenchy" Levent "works rubber" at the annual Christmas circus for the patients at Pacific State Hospital in Pomona, California, sponsored by the Paul Eagles Circus Luncheon Club.

ance of the Circus Vargas I saw under canvas all the clowns had the runs and took turns racing into the arena, doing a quick trick, and racing out again: another example of the audience not realizing what was really going on.

But clowns, in order to survive in the American tradition, need that large base from which to grow; without it, observes Bill Binder, owner-manager of Philippe's in Los Angeles, long-time observer and friend of circus people, "they come out more carny than clown. I hate to see the old clowns die away without being able to pass something on."

So say we all. Perhaps just over the horizon the clown will find himself again in still another incarnation as he has so many times through the centuries. Perhaps television, so starved for stimulating entertainment, will turn to him. Red Skelton is, of course, the obvious example of a tramp-carpet entertaining in that medium, but he had to establish his credentials as a comedy star before being accepted as a clown.

As we have seen, clowns have a great capacity to adapt to time and circumstance. Not too long ago "showing skin," that is, appearing with any part of your skin uncovered by makeup or costume, was considered taboo. Skin meant "human" and the old-time performers understood the need to separate themselves from their audience. Both clowns and circus went to great lengths to preserve the proper image.

Elaborate clown makeup, once applied, was customarily left on all day through the scheduled performances; it was considered in bad taste to appear in public partially out of costume. A clown who wanted to shop in a town and donned his street clothes to do so while leaving on his face was ostracized by both his co-workers and circus management. Referred to contemptuously as a "dirty-neck clown" he either mended his ways or found himself divorced from the company of his fellows until the forced isolation made him quit the show.

Clowns had great dignity, and anything that smacked of carelessness or unseemly behavior reflected on them all and retaliation was often pointed and swift. Discipline is the cement that molds any

art form into a pleasing, finished whole, and the art of clowning appears to be affected by the loss of the arduous training period that leads to a high degree of professionalism.

Whatever the future of the wonderfully resilient clown, for the moment we enjoy him and are grateful for his presence.

"As long," Bobby Kay told me, "as I keep the illusion that I'm not really a man but a clown, I'm happy." The great entertainer cocked his head puckishly to one side. "Because," he said as he smiled and held up an admonishing finger, "remember, a clown is special."

The Russell Brothers Circus, Portland, Oregon, 1942, including a clown gag featuring a live prop and two "exotic" whitefaces.

Making people laugh is hard work. Gene Randow hits the hay while the Big Top fills for the next show.

BIBLIOGRAPHY

Bell, Don. "Sol—Quebec's One-Man Clown Act," *En Route* (December 1974), Volume II, No. 11.

Cahn, William. *A Pictorial History of Great Comedians.* (New York: Grosset and Dunlap, 1957).

Cooper, Courtney Ryley. *Under the Big Top.* (New York: Little, Brown, 1923).

Cornell, Joseph. (Comp.). *Clowns, Elephants and Ballerinas.* (New York: Ballet Caravan, 1946).

Culhane, John. "School For Clowns," *The New York Times Magazine.* (December 30, 1973).

———. "Clown for a Day . . . You Gotta Be Kidding," *Signature* (1974).

Dean, Richard. "The Lore of Harlequin, Pierrot, and Scaramouche," *The Mentor* (December 1924), Volume XXII, No. 11.

Dickens, Charles (Ed.) *Memoirs of Joseph Grimaldi.* (London: 1838).

Disher, M. Willson. *Clowns and Pantomimes.* (London: Constable, 1925). Illustrated.

Duncan, Thomas W. *Gus the Great.* (New York and Philadelphia: Lippincott, 1947).

Fenner, Mildred Sandison and Wolcott (Eds.). *The Circus, Lure and Legend.* (Englewood Cliffs, N.J.: Prentice-Hall, 1970).

Gorham, Maurice. *Showmen and Suckers.* (London: Percival Marshall, 1951). Illustrated by Edward Ardizzone.

Grock (Pseudonym). *King of Clowns.* Written by Adrien Wettach (Grock). Translated by Basil Creighton. (London: Methuen, 1957). Illustrated.

Harzberg, Hiler, and Moss, Arthur. *Slapstick and Dumbbell, A Casual Survey of Clown and Clowning.* (New York: Lawren, 1924). Illustrated.

Hubbard, Freeman. *Great Days of the Circus.* (New York: American Heritage, 1962).

Kelley, Francis Beverly. "The Land of Sawdust and Spangles," *The National Geographic Magazine* (October 1931).

Kelly, Emmett, and Kelley, F. Beverly. *Clown.* (Englewood Cliffs, N.J.: Prentice-Hall, 1954).

Knecht, Klara E. *The Circus Book.* (Akron, Ohio: Saalfield, 1934).

MacKay, Patricia. "Marvelous Magical Mugs for Crazy Comical Clowns," *Theatre Crafts* (September 1972).

Marcks, Don. "The Show Scene," *The Circus Report* (January 6, 1975).

Matthews, Brander. "The Clown in History, Romance and Drama," *The Mentor* (December 1924), Volume XXII, Number 11.

McVicar, J. Wesley. *Clown Act Omnibus.* (New York: Association Press, 1960). Illustrated.

Newton, Douglas. *Clowns.* (New York: Franklin Watts, 1957).

Pfening, Fred D. "The Grand Old Man of the Big Top," *Bandwagon* (September-October 1968).

Popov, Oleg Konstantinovich. *Russian Clown.* Translated by Marion Koenig. (London: Macdonald, 1970). Illustrated.

Rémy, Tristan. *Les Clowns.* (Paris: Grasset, 1945). Illustrated.

Reynolds, Butch. *Broken-Hearted Clown.* (London: Arco Publications, 1954). Illustrated by the author.

Sherwood, Robert Edmund. *Here We Are Again: Recollections of an Old Circus Clown.* (Indianapolis: Bobbs-Merrill, 1926). Illustrated.

Sutton, Felix. *The Book of Clowns.* (New York: Grosset, 1953). Pictures by James Shucker.

Taylor, Robert Lewis. "Family Under Canvas," *The New Yorker Magazine*, (April 23 and 30, 1949).

_____. *Center Ring. The People of the Circus.* (Garden City, N.Y.: Doubleday, 1956).

Wallace, Irving. *The Fabulous Showman. The Life and Times of P. T. Barnum.* (New York: Knopf, 1959).

Willeford, William. *The Fool and His Scepter: A Study in Clowns and Jesters and Their Audience.* (Evanston, Ill.: Northwestern University Press, 1969). Illustrated.

Wilson, A. E. *King Panto, The Story of Pantomime.* (New York: Dutton, 1935). Illustrated.

THE TEXT FOR THIS BOOK WAS SET IN FOURTEEN POINT CALEDONIA,
COMPOSED, PRINTED, AND BOUND BY KINGSPORT PRESS, KINGSPORT, TENNESSEE.
DISPLAY TYPE WAS SET IN EDWARDS AND TUSCAN ORNATE
BY SKIL-SET TYPOGRAPHERS, LOS ANGELES, CALIFORNIA.
BOOK DESIGN BY KADI KARIST TINT.